Time by Design

Design Thinking, Design Theory

Ken Friedman and Erik Stolterman, editors

Design Things, A. Telier (Thomas Binder, Pelle Ehn, Giorgio De Michelis, Giulio Jacucci, Per Linde, and Ina Wagner), 2011

China's Design Revolution, Lorraine Justice, 2012

Adversarial Design, Carl DiSalvo, 2012

The Aesthetics of Imagination in Design, Mads Nygaard Folkmann, 2013

Linkography: Unfolding the Design Process, Gabriela Goldschmidt, 2014

Situated Design Methods, edited by Jesper Simonsen, Connie Svabo, Sara Malou Strandvad, Kristine Samson, Morten Hertzum, and Ole Erik Hansen, 2014

Taking [A]part: The Politics and Aesthetics of Participation in Experience-Centered Design, John McCarthy and Peter Wright, 2015

Design, When Everybody Designs: An Introduction to Design for Social Innovation, Ezio Manzini, 2015

Frame Innovation: Creating New Thinking by Design, Kees Dorst, 2015

Designing Publics, Christopher A. Le Dantec, 2016

Overcrowded: Designing Meaningful Products in a World Awash with Ideas, Roberto Verganti, 2016

FireSigns: A Semiotic Theory for Graphic Design, Steven Skaggs, 2017

Making Design Theory, Johan Redström, 2017

Critical Fabulations: Reworking the Methods and Margins of Design, Daniela Rosner, 2018

Designing with the Body: Somaesthetic Interaction Design, Kristina Höök, 2018

Discursive Design: Critical, Speculative, and Alternative Things, Bruce M. Tharp and Stephanie M. Tharp, 2018

Pretense Design: Surface over Substance, Per Mollerup, 2019

Being and the Screen: How the Digital Changes Perception, Stéphane Vial, 2019

How Artifacts Afford: The Power and Politics of Everyday Things, Jenny L. Davis, 2020

Meaningful Stuff: Design That Lasts, Jonathan Chapman, 2021

Things We Could Design: For More Than Human-Centered Worlds, Ron Wakkary, 2021

The Space Between Look and Read: Designing Complementary Meaning, Susan M. Hagan, 2023

Design, Empathy, Interpretation: Toward Interpretive Design Research, Ilpo Koskinen, 2023

Design Strategy: Challenges in Wicked Problem Territory, Nancy C. Roberts, 2023

Time by Design: How Communicating Slow Allows Us to Go Fast, Dawna I. Ballard, 2025

Time by Design

How Communicating Slow Allows Us to Go Fast

Dawna I. Ballard

The MIT Press

Cambridge, Massachusetts | London, England

The MIT Press
Massachusetts Institute of Technology
77 Massachusetts Avenue, Cambridge, MA 02139
mitpress.mit.edu

The MIT Press would like to thank the anonymous peer reviewers who provided comments on drafts of this book. The generous work of academic experts is essential for establishing the authority and quality of our publications. We acknowledge with gratitude the contributions of these otherwise uncredited readers.

This book was set in Stone Serif and Stone Sans by Westchester Publishing Services. Printed and bound in the United States of America.

Library of Congress Cataloging-in-Publication Data

Names: Ballard, Dawna I. author
Title: Time by design : how communicating slow allows us to go fast / Dawna I. Ballard.
Description: Cambridge, Massachusetts : The MIT Press, [2025] | Series: Design thinking, design theory | Includes bibliographical references and index.
Identifiers: LCCN 2025016513 (print) | LCCN 2025016514 (ebook) | ISBN 9780262552707 paperback | ISBN 9780262383547 pdf | ISBN 9780262383554 epub
Subjects: LCSH: Communication in organizations | Time management | Time—Sociological aspects | Design—Social aspects
Classification: LCC HD30.3 .B367 2025 (print) | LCC HD30.3 (ebook) | DDC 658.4/5—dc23/eng/20250910
LC record available at https://lccn.loc.gov/2025016513
LC ebook record available at https://lccn.loc.gov/2025016514

EU Authorised Representative: Easy Access System Europe, Mustamäe tee 50, 10621 Tallinn, Estonia | Email: gpsr.requests@easproject.com

To Mom and Dad, who taught me why time matters.

Contents

Series Foreword   ix

Acknowledgments   xvii

1   **Time Talks: The Power of Fast and Slow Communication
    Design Logics**   1
2   **Design Frames: Communication and the Designable
    Features of Time**   33
3   **Fast Logics: The Communication Theory of
    More-Faster-Better**   67
4   **Slow Logics: The Communication Theory of Going Slow
    to Go Fast**   113
5   **Beyond Words: Signposts for New Timescapes**   149
6   **Measure Twice: Good Design Takes Time**   165

Notes   183

Index   201

Series Foreword

As professions go, design is relatively young. The practice of design predates professions. In fact, the practice of design—making things to serve a useful goal, making tools—predates the human race. Making tools is one of the attributes that made us human in the first place.

Design, in the most generic sense of the word, began more than two and a half million years ago when *Homo habilis* manufactured the first tools. Human beings were designing well before we began to walk upright. Four hundred thousand years ago, we began to manufacture spears. By forty thousand years ago, we had moved up to specialized tools.

Urban design and architecture came along ten thousand years ago in Mesopotamia. Interior architecture and furniture design probably emerged with them. It was another five thousand years before graphic design and typography got their start in Sumeria with the development of cuneiform. After that, things picked up speed.

All goods and services are designed. The urge to design—to consider a situation, imagine a better situation, and act to create that improved situation—goes back to our prehuman ancestors. Making tools helped us to become what we are: design helped to make us human.

Today, the word "design" means many things. The common factor linking them is service, and designers are engaged in a service profession in which the results of their work meet human needs.

Design is first of all a process. The word "design" entered the English language in the 1500s as a verb, with the first written citation of the verb dated to the year 1548. *Merriam-Webster's Collegiate Dictionary* defines the verb "design" as "to conceive and plan out in the mind; to have as a specific purpose; to devise for a specific function or end." Related to these is the act of drawing, with an emphasis on the nature of the drawing as a plan or map, as well as "to draw plans for; to create, fashion, execute or construct according to plan."

Half a century later, the word began to be used as a noun, with the first cited use of the noun "design" occurring in 1588. *Merriam-Webster's* defines the noun as "a particular purpose held in view by an individual or group; deliberate, purposive planning; a mental project or scheme in which means to an end are laid down." Here, too, purpose and planning toward desired outcomes are central. Among these are "a preliminary sketch or outline showing the main features of something to be executed; an underlying scheme that governs functioning, developing or unfolding; a plan or protocol for carrying out or accomplishing something; the arrangement of elements or details in a product or work of art." Today, we design large, complex process, systems, and services, and we design organizations and structures to produce them. Design has changed considerably since our remote ancestors made the first stone tools.

At a highly abstract level, Herbert Simon's definition covers nearly all imaginable instances of design. To design, Simon writes, is to "[devise] courses of action aimed at changing existing situations into preferred ones" (Simon, *The Sciences of the Artificial*, 2nd ed., MIT Press, 1982, p. 129). Design, properly defined, is the entire process across the full range of domains required for any given outcome.

But the design process is always more than a general, abstract way of working. Design takes concrete form in the work of the service professions that meet human needs, a broad range of making and planning disciplines. These include industrial design, graphic design, textile design, furniture design, information design, process design, product design, interaction design, transportation design, educational design, systems design, urban design, design leadership, and design management, as well as architecture, engineering, information technology, and computer science.

These fields focus on different subjects and objects. They have distinct traditions, methods, and vocabularies, used and put into practice by distinct and often dissimilar professional groups. Although the traditions dividing these groups are distinct, common boundaries sometimes form a border. Where this happens, they serve as meeting points where common concerns build bridges. Today, ten challenges uniting the design professions form such a set of common concerns.

Three performance challenges, four substantive challenges, and three contextual challenges bind the design disciplines and professions together as a common field. The performance challenges arise because all design professions

1. act on the physical world,

2. address human needs, and

3. generate the built environment.

In the past, these common attributes were not sufficient to transcend the boundaries of tradition. Today, objective changes in the larger world give rise to four substantive challenges that are driving convergence in design practice and research. These substantive challenges are:

1. increasingly ambiguous boundaries between artifacts, structure, and process;

2. increasingly large-scale social, economic, and industrial frames;

3. an increasingly complex environment of needs, requirements, and constraints; and

4. information content that often exceeds the value of physical substance.

These challenges require new frameworks of theory and research to address contemporary problem areas while solving specific cases and problems. In professional design practice, we often find that solving design problems requires interdisciplinary teams with a transdisciplinary focus. Fifty years ago, a sole practitioner and an assistant or two might have solved most design problems. Today, we need groups of people with skills across several disciplines and the additional skills that enable professionals to work with, listen to, and learn from each other as they solve problems.

Three contextual challenges define the nature of many design problems today. Although many design problems function at a simpler level, these issues affect many of the major design problems that challenge us, and these challenges also affect simple design problems linked to complex social, mechanical, or technical systems. These issues are:

1. a complex environment in which many projects or products cross the boundaries of several organizations, stakeholder, producer, and user groups;

2. projects or products that must meet the expectations of many organizations, stakeholders, producers, and users; and

3. demands at every level of production, distribution, reception, and control.

These ten challenges require a qualitatively different approach to professional design practice than was the case in earlier times. Past environments were simpler. They made simpler demands. Individual experience and personal development were sufficient for depth and substance in professional practice. Although experience and development are still necessary, they are no longer sufficient. Most of today's design challenges require analytic and synthetic planning skills that cannot be developed through practice alone.

Professional design practice today involves advanced knowledge. This knowledge is not solely a higher level of professional practice. It is also a qualitatively different form of professional practice that emerges in response to the demands of the information society and the knowledge economy to which it gives rise.

In his essay "Why Design Education Must Change" (from *Core77*, November 26, 2010), Donald Norman challenges the premises and practices of the design profession. In the past, designers operated on the belief that talent and a willingness to jump into problems with both feet gives them an edge in solving problems. Norman writes:

> In the early days of industrial design, the work was primarily focused upon physical products. Today, however, designers work on organizational structure and social problems, on interaction, service, and experience design. Many problems involve complex social and political issues. As a result, designers have become applied behavioral scientists, but they are woefully undereducated for the task. Designers often fail to understand the complexity of the issues and the depth of knowledge already known. They claim that fresh eyes can produce novel solutions, but then they wonder why these solutions are seldom implemented, or if implemented, why they fail. Fresh eyes can indeed produce insightful results, but the eyes must also be educated and knowledgeable. Designers often lack the requisite understanding. Design schools do not train students about these complex issues, about the interlocking complexities of human and social behavior, about the behavioral sciences, technology, and business. There is little or no training in science, the scientific method, and experimental design.

This is not industrial design in the sense of designing products but rather industry-related design—design as thought and action for solving problems and imagining new futures. This MIT Press series of books emphasizes strategic design to create value through innovative products and services, and it emphasizes design as service through rigorous creativity, critical inquiry, and an ethics of respectful design. This rests on a sense of understanding, empathy, and appreciation for people, for nature, and for the world we shape through design. Our goal as editors is to develop a series of vital conversations that help designers and researchers to serve business, industry, and the public sector for positive social and economic outcomes.

We will present books that bring a new sense of inquiry to the design, helping to shape a more reflective and stable design discipline able to support a stronger profession grounded in empirical research, generative concepts, and the solid theory that gives rise to what W. Edwards Deming described as profound knowledge (Deming, *The New Economics for Industry, Government, Education*, MIT, Center for Advanced Engineering Study, 1993). For Deming, a physicist, engineer, and designer, profound knowledge comprised systems thinking and the understanding of processes embedded in systems, an understanding of variation and the tools we need to understand variation, a theory of knowledge, and a foundation in human psychology. This is the beginning of "deep design"—the union of deep practice with robust intellectual inquiry.

A series on design thinking and theory faces the same challenges that we face as a profession. On one level, design is a general human process that we use to understand and to shape our world. Nevertheless, we cannot address this process or the world in its general, abstract form. Rather, we meet the challenges of design in specific challenges, addressing problems or ideas in a situated context. The challenges we face as designers today are as diverse as the problems clients bring us. We are involved in design for economic anchors, economic continuity, and economic growth. We design for urban needs and rural needs, for social development and creative communities. We are involved with environmental sustainability and economic policy, agriculture competitive crafts for export, competitive products and brands for micro-enterprises, developing new products for bottom-of-pyramid markets, and redeveloping old products for mature or wealthy markets. Within the framework of design, we are also challenged to design for extreme situations; for biotech, nanotech, and new materials; for social business; as well as for conceptual challenges for worlds that do not yet exist (such as the world beyond the Kurzweil singularity) and for new visions of the world that does exist.

The Design Thinking, Design Theory series from the MIT Press will explore these issues and more—meeting them, examining them, and helping designers to address them.

Join us in this journey.

Ken Friedman
Erik Stolterman
Editors, Design Thinking, Design Theory Series

Acknowledgments

My various observations about the design of time were themselves a slow, gradual process that proceeded in a nonlinear fashion across more than two decades. Yet, it was my work with the Children's Advocacy Centers of Texas (CACTX) that brought these elements into sharp focus. Witnessing their heroic dedication to serve and protect childhood illuminated not just what's possible in work, but what's *essential*. To everyone at CACTX, thank you. Your willingness to share your time and talents with our research team for two years left me deeply indebted. My profound gratitude extends to my core collaborators: Matt McGlone, Mara Waller, Dina Inman, Ana Aguilar, Dron Mandhana, and Estee Solomon Gray. Your brilliant observations, meticulous data collection, and sharp analysis were invaluable. This vital research on behalf of CACTX was made possible by the Texas Children's Justice Act and the National Children's Alliance—thank you for your support.

In addition to my work with CACTX, other scholarly collaborations described in these pages helped me to understand how slow is fast (and why fast is often slow). To Yoram Kalman, thank you for leading our exploration of chronemic urgency. My sincere thanks to Urmimala Sakar, M.D. and Mike Pignone, M.D. for your insights and help in assembling such an incredible research team to study time in primary care: Elizabeth Jacobs, M.D., Kate Sebastian, R.N., M.P.H., Michelle-Linh Nguyen, M.D., Ana Aguilar, Deepak Maharaj, D.O., and Anastajza Harris. To the clinicians that shared so freely and permitted us to shadow their work, thank you. Harry Edwards, exploring the world of American football was enriched by your generous feedback and guidance. Additional thanks goes to the sports professionals and players who shared their stories with us, my research team (Dina Inman, Sunshine Webster, Dave Bryant, Kristin Green, Pauline Mar, Nathaniel "Tre" Newton, Sarah Sparks, Jason Flowers, Ashley Barrett, Sarah Rogers, Carley Whitson, and Leah Brisco) who made this impressive array of interviews possible, Chris Hart for his support of the project, and the Center for Sports Communication & Media for funding this endeavor. To Victor Montori, M.D., whose research I drew on before we ever met, it has been a delight to collaborate in measuring unhurried conversations. Thank you to the entire scale development team (Dron Mandhana, Cristian Soto Jacome, M.D., Sarah Johnson, Yohanna Tesfai, Michael Gionfriddo, Nataly Espinoza Suarez, M.D., and Lillian Su, M.D.) for their insights and analyses.

My understanding of design benefitted from multiple conversations with Mark Aakhus and Josh Barbour—thank you both for your encouragement. Tom McVey, your writing and enthusiasm about design sparked my initial curiosity in this field, leading me to Mark's powerful work on communication-as-design. Betelhem Makonnen, your transcendent art became integral to this book. Not only did you generously allow its inclusion, but your *Rock Standard Time (RST)* exhibit beautifully captured the essence of my fieldwork. I am grateful to the wonderful team at the MIT Press who brought *Time by Design* into being. While many contributed, I want to especially thank Ken Friedman, Erik Stolterman, and Noah Springer for your early belief in these ideas and for including the book in the Design Thinking, Design Theory series.

This book found its footing during a Provost's Authors Fellowship filled with the early and ongoing support of Mounira (Maya) Charrad, Dhiraj Murthy, Kirsten "Kit" Belgum, and Jennifer Wilks—thank you. The magnificent design work and feedback from Dave McClinton, along with the brilliant editing, cheerleading, and problem-solving by Kerby Caudill (and Jeff Caudill when needed), made this work (and my life) immeasurably better and easier. Thank you to Larry Browning, Brenda Allen, Rod Hart, Keri Stephens, Craig Scott, Ursula Ballard, Cherise Smith, Christine Moline, Cathy Walker, DeMethra "Sha" Bradley, Yohanna Tesfai, Kennedy Freyer, Jenny Nguyen, Jennifer Betancourt, and Lisa Moseley—your help navigating various aspects of this book's creation is deeply appreciated.

Finally, the daily rhythms and interactions with my husband, Joe, my mother, Anita, and my daughter, Lela Day, served as constant, beautiful reminders that time is, indeed, by design. I am endlessly grateful for the time we share and your unwavering love and support.

1

Time Talks: The Power of Fast and Slow Communication Design Logics

Time talks.

—Edward T. Hall

The efficiency of symbols, as a means of communication and coordination, can be associated with the power to do more than just *mean* this or that. Symbols can be experienced as if they, in fact, *are* this or that. Time-keeping technologies such as clocks, calendars, schedules, and even the week are incredibly effective tools at hiding the thing they are designed to symbolize. Their design is more than merely efficient. In contemporary Western postindustrial culture, these designs drive powerful communication media that shape the most important aspects of our lives. Indeed, in the first sentence of his first (and widely influential) book *The Silent Language*, cultural anthropologist Edward T. Hall states simply, "Time talks."[1] Clocks literally "tell" us the time, our alarms wake us from sleep, calendars let us know the day, our schedules signal what we should be doing, and deadlines demand our attention—all the while excluding a whole range of other human activity.

On the surface, this mistaking of time for the symbolic designs that help us communicate about time might seem to be of little consequence. However, this misunderstanding has far-reaching implications for our personal and professional lives. In equating time with a clock, we have imbued time with a variety of machine-like qualities and traits that are in stark contrast to the contours and inner workings of human bodies, human relationships, and the whole of human lives. We ask of ourselves to produce more, faster, and better—something that machines are designed and then redesigned to do. Google N-gram notes that this phrase, "more-faster-better," first appeared around 1976 and has become increasingly popular since the turn of the century.

All of this in spite of the reality: We are time. We create it. We are bound by a design of our own making. Physicists can find no evidence of this thing we call "time." Time is ours. This is the focus of chronemics—that is, time as it is bound to human communication.[2] In *Time by Design*, I draw upon more than two decades of my research to explore the underlying chronemic designs that shape time in our work, relationships, and communities and offer a toolkit to create time differently. Although the designable features of time are often hidden, I use wide-ranging examples and case studies to reveal how this process unfolds in everyday communication norms in both personal and professional settings. Accordingly, I take a transdisciplinary approach that goes beyond any one discipline— for example, medicine, art, management, sociology, psychology, communication, and design—to explore the underlying commonalities about time to which they all point.

Time by Design has two central aims. One is to identify and demonstrate the importance of two underlying communication design logics (CDLs)—that is, fast and slow—that illustrate how effective teams, communities, and organizations routinely communicate slow to go fast. The other is to share a practical toolkit needed for doing the real, often difficult, work of designing times that ultimately deliver speed outside of limited, linear, transactional industrial-era strategies (i.e., more-faster-better). I illustrate how people, groups, and organizations thrive in contemporary life through attention to expanded time frames, nonlinear trajectories, and the possibilities for transcendence that communication holds. *Time by Design* is a blueprint for doing so.

Notably, given the long-standing interest regarding time in the practice of design,[3] this book is about the work of design as much as it is about the design itself. "Measure twice, cut once," a carpentry aphorism, reflects an inherent tension addressed throughout: Good design takes time. Although I reflect on this issue at length in the concluding chapter, the normative claim that both fast and slow CDLs must be used together in a complementary fashion applies to the process of design as well as the team, community, or organizational communication processes being designed.

Designing Time, Navigating Temporality

The 2017 Nobel Prize in Physiology or Medicine was awarded for the discovery of the biological clock. In their press release, the recipients Jeffrey C. Hall, Michael Rosbash, and Michael W. Young cautioned, "Chronic misalignment between our lifestyle and the rhythm dictated by our inner timekeeper is associated with increased risk for various diseases."[4] This concern with finding our rhythm is fundamentally an issue of bringing our *time* into alignment with our biological *temporality*. That is, although the "times" of our lives—our work, our social media, our cultural norms—are the product of human design, our biological clocks are not. We are temporal beings. We design time. The Nobel laureates' charge is for humans to better design their times around temporality.

Temporality refers to the inherent patterns that define a process, event, or activity. This includes birth, death, and the diurnal cycle (i.e., a tuner for our biological clock) that drives everything in between. Organizational attention to temporality includes an implicit understanding that some things take their "own time," such as engaged conversations, learning curves, phases of problem solving, and the development of team cohesion and relationships. Rather than being organically tied to time, work naturally unfolds through multiple temporal processes. All human processes are temporal, including communication.

Time, in contrast, refers to the various symbolic external markers that point toward those processes and activities. For instance, we use reminder alarms to interrupt our conversations and signal an upcoming meeting. The days of the week pace our activities.[5] Shared holidays signal (potential) moments away from work.[6] Fundamentally, these interventions are time: organizing technologies co-constructed by people via their interactions and formalized through the use of symbols. We communicate using a variety of technologies—from simple to complex—that hold presumptions about time and, in turn, have important consequences for human activity. These technologies are not all machines. They range from atomic clocks and international time zones to project deadlines and weekly schedules.

Betelhem Makonnen's 2020 prize-winning exhibition, *Rock Standard Time (RST)*, exemplifies the complex and contested interrelationships between time and temporality. She writes:

> The exhibited works in *Rock Standard Time (RST)* offer perceptual tools and references for those looking to conjugate their present, collapse their tenses–remembering that both the past and future coexist in this moment. By shifting perspective, we can acknowledge the different scales for counting time—universe, stars, planet, rock, tree, human civilization, documented history—down to the years, days, and seconds of a single human lifetime. Time is always a reference to something else, so choose your reference carefully.

> *Rock Standard Time (RST)* is a zone to res(e)t your clock and
> consider that we are part of time ourselves so time has to be on
> our side. It's up to us to take a radical leap refusing obedience to
> the accelerated ticking that has us convinced we have no time to
> respond to ourselves, to each other, nor our world.

Makonnen and I scheduled a public conversation about her exhibition in March 2020. Of course, it was canceled based on a temporal event—a global pandemic—but many months later, she arranged a private viewing for me at the Big Medium art gallery.[7]

A multidisciplinary artist, Makonnen is a native of Ethiopia living in Austin, and she brings the times of these two places (and more) together in her work. Several weeks before her exhibition opened, we met for lunch across from the gallery at the suggestion of art historian Cherise Smith, our mutual colleague and friend, who saw several points of overlap in our research and practice. I quickly discovered that Makonnen's understanding of time as designed was grounded in the very practical, lived reality of interacting with family and friends across two cultures and continents. She talked about communicating and translating between two different calendars (Ethiopian and US) on a daily basis—one with thirteen months (the Ethiopian calendar is in sync with the solar cycle) and the other (US) with twelve, one that begins in what Americans view as the ninth month (September) and the other in January, one where the year was 2012 when we first met and the other where it was 2020 (based on different calculations between the two as to the birth of Jesus). This designed nature of time comes through in her work, and it points to (even shouts at) the often unacknowledged possibilities for redesign.

Rock Standard Time (RST) features eleven works curated amid stark white gallery walls with ample white space—all of which Makonnen uses strategically to create a contemplative pace for visitors. The art itself ranges from photography to sculpture to video installations and even "gallery space prep" (golden hour light, conjugated now, tenacity, and resilience) made up of vinyl window tint, wall clocks, and succulent plants. Throughout, she contrasts time and temporality, illustrating how our time use reflects one design among many. For instance, her video installation *untitled (anti-productivity exercises or moving time and space)* speaks to the relationship between time and temporality in design work and especially the idea that good design takes time (issues addressed at length in chapters 2 and 6). It features Makonnen iteratively arranging and rearranging rocks "just so" in the manner of a designer working patiently and earnestly to get it right. Her back-and-forth movement marked by a deeply contented look filled with both uncertainty and patience appears as an exercise in what designers Harold G. Nelson and Erik Stolterman call "design wisdom." Elaborated at length in chapters 5 and 6, design wisdom asks that we take a measured path to properly join both time-based (digital) and temporal (analog) activities.

Her sculptural use of rocks of varied scales and sizes to juxtapose the temporality of rocks against our human time-keeping devices is particularly illustrative here. This includes the *anti-exhaustion wristwatch (monitors naps taken, long meals shared, climbing nothing, dream rate, and more)* (see figure 1.1) that uses small, tumbled rocks (i.e., representing temporality) to obscure the face of the watch (i.e., representing time). Among other things, the *anti-exhaustion wristwatch* suggests that quantitative measurement designs are limited in their ability to account for the qualitative nature of human temporal experience. Each of the activities it "monitors" are temporally, not time, bound. The *time* of an activity is a fungible marker used to point toward an activity, whereas its *temporality* is epochal, emergent through the activity itself.[8] Although naps, meals, climbs, and dreams can be timed with a functional timepiece, they can (and Makonnen suggests *should*) also be enjoyed completely outside of time.

The normative claim running throughout the photography, video, text, and installations that make up *Rock Standard Time (RST)*

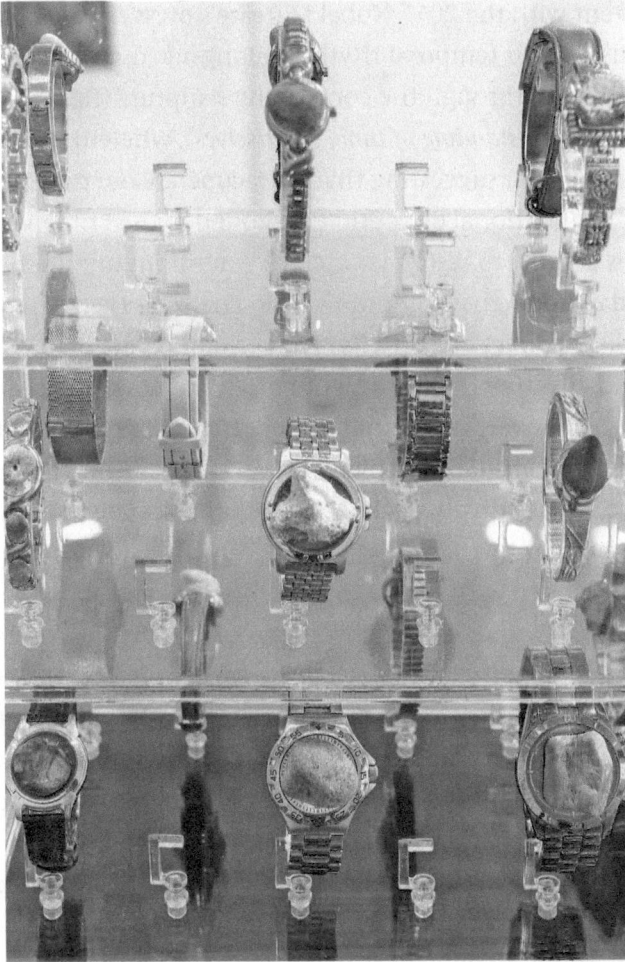

Figure 1.1
Betelhem Makonnen, *anti-exhaustion wristwatch (monitors naps taken, long meals shared, climbing nothing, dream rate, and more)*, 2020.

is consistent with the 2017 Nobel laureate's press release counseling us to consider our temporal rhythms alongside our time demands.[9] It is highlighted through the contrasting sculpture (figure 1.2), *untitled (our misunderstanding of time, of ourselves)*, wherein wristwatches are worn by rocks, suggesting that we recuperate our own temporality as the foundational driver that uses our designed timepieces. The exhibit as a "zone to res(e)t your clock" questions our uncritical use of everyday nonverbal communication channels (i.e., wristwatches and clocks) to direct our activity. These channels are extraordinarily useful and effective in directing our attention toward linear, short-term, quantitatively measurable, and transactional activities. As *Rock Standard Time (RST)* depicts, however, attention to nonlinear, long-term, qualitatively reckoned, and transcendent activities is equally important.

As I mentioned with regard to our scheduled talk about *Rock Standard Time (RST)*, one extreme example of the distinction between time and temporality arose during the early days and weeks of the COVID-19 pandemic: Many people were largely without time in their work. Work became temporal—adapting to the global event we collectively faced. Important meetings, conferences, and production schedules were canceled. Time-keeping devices lost a great deal of agency. Some of our work was still largely tied to time (e.g., mail delivery), and even that failed in many ways (e.g., there were regular delays and shipping slowdowns because of the pandemic). For many, work was tied to the temporality of sheltering in place. We had to reimagine and redesign work without notice or planning: without time. Our lives became a hybrid of the most exigent aspects of pre-industrial, event-based, temporality and postindustrial, always on, timeless time.[10] The pandemic had devastating consequences and is certainly not a model of sustainable work. Nonetheless, these sort of catastrophic events (e.g., pandemics, wars, natural disasters) are rare moments when even members of contemporary Western culture are collectively reminded that work is not organically tied to time.

Figure 1.2
Betelhem Makonnen, *untitled (our misunderstanding of time, of ourselves)*, 2020.

Outside of catastrophic events, the challenge in maintaining both time and temporality in our daily activities is that the speed offered by narrowing our focus exclusively on time is contagious.[11] Thomas Hylland Eriksen, a social anthropologist, argues that "slow" is the primary scarce resource in the twenty-first century, and as such, it must be guarded. His critique is consistent with sociologist Max Weber's early twentieth-century prediction that the efficiency of modern industrialization would become a *stahlhartes gehäuse*, or "iron cage" as it was later translated.[12] Research across disciplines illustrates how relying solely upon time, to the exclusion of temporal processes, puts organizations and their members at risk. Across literatures, it is associated with lower performance,[13] overwork,[14] and burnout.[15] In contrast, a temporally informed perspective is associated with stronger performance, improved communication, and greater resilience—even in the most time-constrained and demanding organizational environments.[16]

The focus of *Time by Design* is to consider ways that communication-as-design offers a path to leverage the value of both time and temporality in our work. Communication-as-design refers to the interventions in human activity that enable certain forms of communication and avoid others.[17] Distinct from the communication design discipline, communication-as-design is a theoretical perspective on the ways people use communication to achieve the ordinary and extraordinary in their day-to-day interactions. It concerns how communication is a design to hold conversations, to organize collectives, and to accomplish any number of personal and professional goals.

My use of communication-as-design in *Time by Design* is in conversation with the larger field of design, including the discipline of communication design. At least as early as the 1980s, *Design Studies* published research and commentary that considered the temporal aspects of design work.[18] These concerns around time and temporality have been largely unaddressed in a systematic way. Yet, they may be even more relevant today. By articulating the unique value of a communication lens on the design process, *Time by Design* accomplishes two things. It offers a fresh approach for academics, practicing professionals, and a general readership to understand time through its integrative and transdisciplinary approach. It also addresses a challenge for mainstream design itself: managing the tension between time and temporality in design work. Below, I elaborate the interrelationship among design, time, and temporality using the three starting points for those wishing to engage in communication-as-design work proposed by communication scholars Mark Aakhus and Sally Jackson: (1) design is a natural fact about communication, (2) designs are hypotheses, and (3) design is theoretical.[19]

Communication as a Design for Time

I wrote part of this book during a yearlong writing fellowship at the University of Texas at Austin. The innovation of the particular fellowship I was awarded (i.e., the Provost's Authors Fellowship) is that it leveraged three things—time, money, and communication—to help faculty finish books that they will otherwise find difficult to complete amid so many other competing demands. It gave *time* by cutting faculty's teaching load in half. It gave *money* through a partial summer salary and a small budget to help pay for research expenses (i.e., travel, books, software, etc.) so that faculty are less inclined to seek money (and spend time) elsewhere (e.g., summer school or consulting gigs).

These two resources are wonderful yet not particularly unusual or rare on their own. Nevertheless, marshaling these resources together along with the third resource, *communication*, is the key design feature that ably supported the goals of the fellowship. Faculty were assigned to small groups of five and were required to meet monthly and circulate their work with each other (in advance) for feedback and discussion. Our meetings tended to last about two hours and often went longer. This is a lot of time in a busy week, and I (and other colleagues in the group) initially feared it would offset some of the perks by consuming valuable time. We were mistaken. As our one of our meetings was ending (having collectively decided on a date for the next one), my colleague exhaled, "Great—it will force me to get my work done!"

This reflected communication-as-design, as Aakhus describes "an intervention into some ongoing activity through the invention of techniques, devices, and procedures that aim to redesign interactivity and thus shape the possibilities for communication."[20] Specifically, this was a communication design for time. The power of a shared date and time on the calendar to focus and drive human activity is remarkable. We know this instinctively (and so, for many groups and organizations, meetings proliferate and, ironically, become ineffective). The commitment to share this date and time and to be in conversation with each other (i.e., accountable to others) is the experience to which my colleague was pointing.

Notably, it is not the calendar alone but also a particular quality about the relationship *between* time and communication that actually drives task accomplishment. This quality is "recursivity," which can be described as the chicken-and-the-egg problem: Each one shapes and is shaped by the other to such an extent that it is not useful (or even possible) to say which came first or which one causally influences the other.[21] Instead, we consider them as arising together (i.e., mutually constituted), with each having direct consequences for the other. This is why communication scholar Thomas Bruneau defined chronemics as the study of time as it is bound to communication. This recursive relationship is also reflected in sociologist Émile Durkheim's observation that "a calendar expresses the rhythm of the collective activities, while at the same time its function is to assure its regularity."[22] The calendar has an expressive quality that regulates time through symbolizing it—thus, these two processes are bound together.

More fundamentally, in *Outline of a Theory of Practice*,[23] French sociologist Pierre Bourdieu observed that time (not temporality) only came into being as early humans interacted with each other, noticing that others were present in some moments and not in others. Ultimately, in the desire to intervene in this flow of presence and absence, such as to interact with others or to avoid interaction, time was born. Thus, time is an everyday communication intervention designed to regulate temporal processes. It enables and constrains communication. It directs our attention to certain interactions and away from others in every given moment. This occurs on a large scale in organizational and institutional contexts as well as in everyday interpersonal interactions. Figure 1.3 depicts this recursive relationship: Human interaction brings time into being, and the designable features of time are then used (purposefully or accidentally) to shape the communication that is likely to occur.

Returning to our calendar example, time is used to design one's availability, as in the case of shared calendaring systems indicating when one is free for interaction. Scheduled appointments on that same calendaring system indicate one's lack of availability to others

Figure 1.3
The recursive relationship between time and communication.

outside of the appointment. Further, incessant attention to one's wristwatch during that appointment is a common (although not universal) gesture to signify the desired end of interaction (either because the meeting is running long or because of general disinterest). Finally, keeping someone waiting, effectively delaying that scheduled appointment, is experienced as conveying a lack of regard by individuals in some cultures.[24]

However, there is another critical relationship between time and communication—that is, the focus of *Time by Design*—that can be leveraged to improve organizational processes: Communication-as-design can be used to fashion collective time in support of temporal processes. The answer to a common question I receive from entrepreneurs, managers, and other business professionals I meet offers an example. I am routinely asked: With the availability of vastly improved videoconferencing (even telepresence robots), is face-to-face communication and the related travel it entails still a worthwhile investment? The answer I give is yes, particularly depending upon the stage of their current project, the type of project, and how long the team has been working together. This is because face-to-face communication readily facilitates temporal processes that typically do not unfold well in the time allotted for videoconference calls.

A leading communication scholar in the area of supercomputing and cyberinfrastructure adoption, Kerk Kee, studies this very question. Contrary to stereotypes about scientists being interested only in efficiency and time-saving, Kee finds that effective virtual organizations require colocated meetings prior to the start of the collaboration and periodically after that point.[25] Scientists and administrators alike told Kee's research team that taking the time to make the trip, which frequently requires international travel, is critical to the success of their collaborations. It is time-consuming, expensive, and inefficient from a short-term, linear perspective. Nonetheless, spending several days together, involved in off-topic conversation and mundane interpersonal settings, builds trust and gives members a relational context with which to interpret future messages. Therefore, it is quite effective from a long-term, nonlinear perspective. Administrators offered, "We will get together for that kick-off meeting. We'll do that in person because there's no substitute for getting to know somebody, seeing the body language, [and] being able to work on a white board . . . [Y]ou don't build relationships with purely Skype calls or video conferencing."[26]

There are also technical learning processes that benefit from the design of colocated activities. An administrator and technology developer explained: "The technology developer spent a day in the clinic and saw what it was like . . . That was super enlightening for us. Because we could immediately see—Gosh, this is taking way longer than it should. Why is it taking so long?—It's for a variety of reason[s], but it helped us understand what the workflow was [like]."[27] These multidisciplinary teams (MDTs) of individuals from different institutions rely so heavily on trust (that develops through varied communication processes) that Kee and his colleagues modify the pop-culture phrase "If you build it, they will come" to "If you build it, promote it, and they trust you, then they will come" to underscore the centrality of communication to their successes.

To summarize Kee's findings, an engineer who works in outreach explained, "It's not just solving a technical problem with cyberinfrastructure, it's the engagement . . . between cyberinfrastructure engineers and team members and the researchers . . . We're going to personally, constructively engage with researchers and kind of do the legwork to *build relationships* and relationships of trust."[28] The common metaphorical usage of design terms such as "building" relationships, "forming" coalitions, or "forging" friendships suggests that communication-as-design is key to effective work and that we, routinely in the course of our everyday lives, are all designers. These efforts reflect the first starting point for communication-as-design offered by Aakhus and Jackson: Design is a natural fact about communication.[29]

Design as a natural fact about communication indicates that all communication is designed. Kee's administrators and computer scientists articulated this basic principle of communication-as-design by describing their strategies to build trusting relationships that assist their work objectives. Makonnen drew attention to the design of timepieces as powerful pacers for human activity. Similarly, one aim of *Time by Design* is to identify the everyday chronemic designs that have important (i.e., positive and negative) consequences for collectives' ability to respond successfully to urgent time demands on an ongoing basis. The second aim is to offer a Chronemic Design Toolkit that can be used to support a range of temporally driven communication processes. The two chronemic designs at the center of discussion are not intended to be exhaustive, as the number of design possibilities for a given situation is limitless. Rather, these designs are elaborated in order to draw attention to common beliefs about the relationship between time and communication and to consider their consequences based on empirical evidence.

Drawing from a range of organizational settings and projects, I have observed varied communication interventions designed to bend and (re)form time to meet the needs of individuals, teams, and organizations. These interventions reflect the second principle of a communication-as-design enterprise: Designs are hypotheses. Professional designers and organizational members alike test varied hypotheses about how communication works best in the face of continually urgent time demands. The hypotheses are revealed in the diverse contours, or dimensions, of time made to reshape how communication functions. These hypotheses are based on underlying theories of communication, reflecting the third principle of a communication design enterprise: Design is theoretical. When it comes to design intended to aid time-sensitive interaction, these distinct theories refer only to beliefs about how to design *communication*, not the broader work activity. As I explain in the next section, the ultimate goal of both fast and slow communication design is the same: Respond quickly to time demands as they arise. Each is outlined below and elaborated in the remainder of the book.

Fast and Slow Communication Design Logics

In the organizations I have studied, the range of design approaches I have observed embody two fundamentally different theories of how communication works in fast-paced work environments. Table 1.1 summarizes what I will elaborate in the pages that follow.

First, the conventional approach designs communication to conform to and *fit around existing time constraints*. The theory here is that a quickly changing environment requires fast communication design. "Fast" refers to what communication is designed to

Table 1.1
Two contrasting approaches to chronemic design

Fast Communication Design Logics	Slow Communication Design Logics
Overall Design Approach	
Communication begins with time	Communication begins with temporality
Time based	Process based
Communication fits the time: communication processes must fit into available time	Time fits the communication: time is designed to include communication processes
Time is a primary means of task accomplishment	Relationships are a primary means of task accomplishment
Underlying Theories About Communication	
Unfolds in a single frame of interaction	Unfolds over multiple frames of interaction
Has a linear relationship with time: communication costs time	Has a nonlinear relationship with time: communication saves time
Interaction is transactional	Interaction is transcendent

accomplish: speed up to keep up. This is epitomized in the common idiom "We're building the car while we're driving it." The presumption is that if the organizational environment is fast, the only way to survive is to design communication that can outrun the speed of change in the environment. This preoccupation with speed is tied to an implicit belief that time is the primary means of task accomplishment. As will be explained further in chapter 4, this belief is historically and geographically unique—born of the industrial era.

The alternative approach designs communication to contain and *make room for temporal processes that alter existing time constraints.* The theory here is that a quickly changing environment requires slow communication design. Again, "slow" refers to the pace of communication: pause regularly to regroup and go faster. As elaborated at length in chapter 4, this practice is tied to an implicit belief that relationships, developed through interaction, are a primary means of task accomplishment.

To continue the car metaphor in the idiom above, slow communication design begins with a well-designed car and includes regular stops to refuel and check oil levels to avoid any unnecessary delays. The logic here is that since a fast communication environment never stops, communication-as-design should compel organizational members to routinely pause so that they communicate more effectively, thereby improving performance and avoiding mistakes that are especially costly *because* things never slow down. Slow communication design follows the admonition of John Wooden, highly celebrated basketball coach of the UCLA Bruins nicknamed the Wizard of Westwood, who held an eighty-eight-game winning streak, earned ten national championships (seven in a row) over twelve years, and was named national coach of the year six times: "If you don't have time to do it right, when will you have time to do it over?"

Slow communication design is distinct from the worldwide slow movement, which includes areas of activism such as slow design.[30] It is not a philosophy to guide and reshape *how design works* (although it has implications for the work of design that I elaborate briefly below, further in chapter 2, and underscore in chapter 6). It is an articulation of a set of design principles about *how communication works* to help groups and organizations respond to the time-sensitive demands they face. Because these principles are often implicit and unconscious, I begin by identifying the underlying theories of communication upon which a given design is based. These designs can then be leveraged as an intervention in the service of particular goals.

Although slow communication design is not part of the slow movement, various enterprises such as slow design or slow science, for instance, may reflect underlying slow CDLs. Additionally, my use of the term "slow" is consistent with and draws from Carlo Petrini's—the movement's originator—use of the term. Despite common misperceptions, the aim of the slow food movement was not simply to reduce one's speed.[31] Importantly, Petrini never advocated that all meals be slow. His focus in the slow food movement was that communities reclaim the choice to decide when to go slow or go fast (i.e., *tempo giusto*; right speed). Notably, the advocated shift from fast food to home-cooked meals with one's family was not about the amount of time taken by the activity but rather about the temporal processes allowed to unfold when one prepares food and sits down to eat with others.

Similarly, taking time to communicate supports processes—including relationship development, learning, recovery—that ultimately allow people to work faster and more effectively.[32] Despite this evidence, various forms of slow communication design are often resisted.[33] The classical school of management that originated in the late nineteenth century and early twentieth century as part of the Industrial Revolution trained people to believe that communication should be avoided in general, and especially in time-sensitive settings, because it slowed action,[34] reflecting a conventional fast CDL. In the last century, this fast CDL led to the proliferation of larger and larger employee manuals filled with standard operating procedures, rules, and regulations for every conceivable situation so that communication could (in theory) be minimized.

In contemporary organizations, however, the limitations of this approach have become more obvious, given the rise of interaction work identified by the McKinsey Global Institute more than a decade ago.[35] In twenty-first-century work, we see that communication and relationships are central to getting work done. Yet, the early suspicion that communication is costly (because of the time investment it incurs) still exists. It is managed by trying to fit in more communication faster to compensate for the time it takes: Rather than limiting the *amount of communication* (as a twentieth-century classical approach to management would counsel), the *amount of time* devoted to a given communication demand is limited. It expressly speeds up communication because pace is defined as the number of inputs per unit of time.

For example, fast communication design leads to a larger number of short customer service calls and brief doctor's visits (both of which involve navigating potentially complex communication needs) alongside voluminous email messages (which involve simplifying communication needs). Although these emails, calls, and visits may be fast in some regards (i.e., written quickly or finished swiftly), they often take considerable time to be deciphered. As a result, the theory of fast communication may lead to slower communication when viewed at a system level.

Throughout this introductory chapter, I have referenced three underlying theories of communication that distinguish between fast versus slow CDLs. They reflect elements of communication that fundamentally design time. Three questions help to discern whether a particular design strategy relies upon speeding up communication or slowing it down to have greater impact:

1. What is the time frame of the interaction?
2. What is the perceived shape of the trajectory between time and interaction?
3. What is the underlying belief about what interaction offers?

As these questions suggest, fast communication and slow communication are neither binary descriptors nor on a simple continuum. The logics are constituted through multiple design elements that reflect beliefs, or theories, about how time-sensitive communication is accomplished in a given setting. Each communicator brings with them lay theories that provide an answer to each of these questions. Note that the answers change depending on the temporal demands of the setting. Figure 1.4 depicts each of the elements addressed, in turn, below.

1.   What Is the Time Frame of the Interaction?

All communication implies and involves negotiating a time frame for interaction.[36] We can use the first set of figures in figure 1.4 to visually consider these time frames. Where the double-arrowed lines represent all possibilities for interaction across time, our actual communication serves to bracket, or punctuate, our attention. We can focus narrowly on a single frame of interaction or we can include multiple frames. One way to assess the time frame of a given interaction is to consider whether the past, present, and future are invoked in some way. For instance, a morning hello while ordering breakfast at a local diner has cultural norms that shape its time frame, but it is also negotiated in the moment between two people. Will it simply be contained by a "thank you" and a smile? Will you linger and chat because you are a regular there and the place is empty? Or are you new to the establishment and have lots of questions? As we look more closely, this example shows that

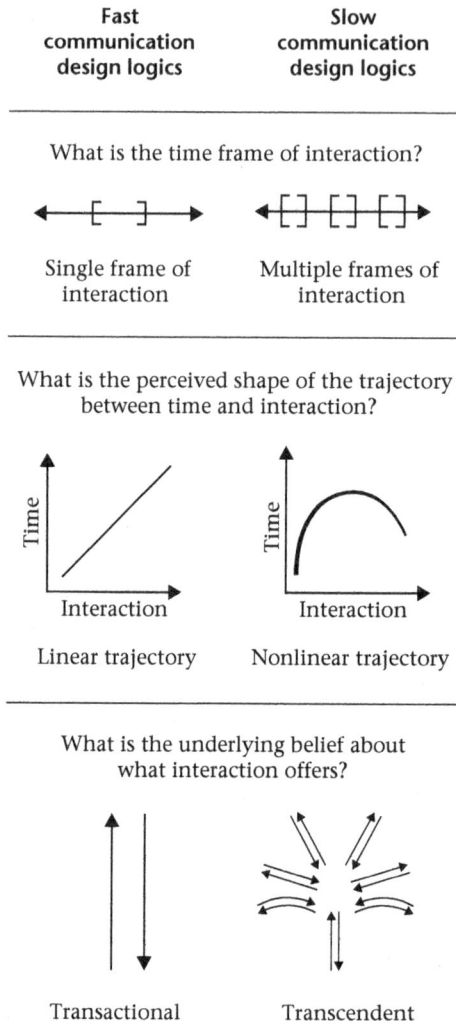

Fast communication design logics	Slow communication design logics

What is the time frame of interaction?

Single frame of interaction	Multiple frames of interaction

What is the perceived shape of the trajectory between time and interaction?

Linear trajectory	Nonlinear trajectory

What is the underlying belief about what interaction offers?

Transactional	Transcendent

Figure 1.4
The three elements of fast and slow communication design logics.

not only does interaction always contain a given time frame but also it can unfold in a singular frame or through multiple distinct time frames that orient participants toward the past, present, and/ or future. Accordingly, fast and slow communication design can be differentiated by the time frames that characterize interaction. The *Rock Standard Time (RST)* exhibition described earlier highlights the importance of framing time in and through our communication norms and habits.

In fast communication design, there is less interest in past time frames (i.e., experiences that help shape how an individual, group, or organization came to be) and future time frames (i.e., how the current interaction shapes what comes next). Fast communication design is generally oriented toward a single frame (i.e., the present) and may overlook historical context (i.e., the past) or distant goals (i.e., the future) in the process of rushing to task completion. In contrast, slow communication design may rely upon all three time frames and use this more expansive framing to inform the interaction. To extend the example of getting breakfast at a local diner, regular waitstaff who know your order without you saying a word are, in that interaction, invoking the past. This frame saves them time during a hectic breakfast hour and speeds things along. It is based on a relationship and rapport that you developed in the past that you continue to develop during each interaction (i.e., present), and it suggests the hope of future interaction to come. Talking with new customers will take longer, but if they continue to patronize the establishment and develop a relationship with those in the organization, all three frames may be eventually developed, offering more context and affording greater speed of interaction. Additionally, if waitstaff spend more time catching up with established customers during slower times of the day, these frames continually expand.

In many organizational settings, invoking multiple time frames need not involve the same two people but can refer to the general relationship between an organization and its public (including

clients, suppliers, and other stakeholders). For example, various airline personnel at an international airport may be singularly focused
on one task and one time frame in a given interaction. However,
their work may still be designed as part of a larger interaction that
reaches back to the past and extends into the future. The very idea
of frequent flyer programs is based on invoking a shared past, present, and future. A number of courtesies (such as early boarding and
first-class upgrades) implicitly refer to a shared past that is used to
support a greater ease of travel for customers in that category. Perks
and privileges designed for some customers and not others do not
shape the broader organizational time frame. However, they highlight how communication design logics can be used to draw on
multiple time frames.

The time frame of an interaction is not necessarily tied to its
duration. Research on trauma resuscitation teams led by Dr. Lillian
Su, a pediatric cardiologist at Phoenix Children's Hospital, found
that even a modest time frame expansion can support task coordination and performance. Using a simulation exercise, her research
team found that communication during the brief moments spent
waiting in the trauma bay (i.e., on average only two minutes) predicted how efficiently surgical teams coordinated after the patient
arrived.[37] Teams who freely participated in shared conversation
before the patient arrived (rather than the head physician simply talking at the others) were able to establish communication
norms that helped them during the resuscitation. The teams who
participated in conversation in the trauma bay were able to anticipate each other's needs and behaviors after the patient arrived and
dynamically adjust their behavior in response, without a spoken
word and without a plan. These team members were more likely
to anticipate the needs of their colleagues and *proactively volunteer*
information such as "Blood pressure is sixty over thirty-six" without being asked.[38]

This is an example of how multiple time frames can be embedded in even the shortest period of time. The entire interaction only lasted about seven minutes on average, but we can see an immediate past (chatting in the trauma bay), present (engaged in resuscitation based on unfolding patient vitals), and future (anticipating what will be needed to support the resuscitation as it progresses) within that brief window. By comparison, teams where the head physician did most of the talking while waiting in the trauma bay spent more time after the patient arrived reactively asking and answering questions. For instance, they *asked* team members, "Do you hear breath sounds?" and needed to wait for an answer to inform their decision-making.[39] In effect, they remained focused on a singular time frame (reacting only to what was happening in a given moment) but without the added resource of temporal context that helped team members anticipate each other's needs. Thus, the time spent engaged in conversation before the patient arrived saved time later, which supported their efficiency and effectiveness.

2.   What Is the Perceived Shape of the Trajectory Between Time and Interaction?

As time frames expand, the perceived relationship between time and interaction (i.e., its trajectory) tends to shift as well. This is the second element that differentiates fast and slow communication design logics. Because more limited time frames constrain the larger arc of events and exclude so many temporal patterns, the relationship between time and communication appears *linear*. Note the steady incremental diagonal line graph in figure 1.4 that depicts what more communication does in terms of time (i.e., it costs time in a never-ending linear relationship). In contrast, larger time frames offer more data points that reveal a *nonlinear* relationship between time and communication. Note the classic inverted U-shaped line graph in figure 1.4 that depicts—at a certain point—what more communication does in terms of time. This understanding is vital in shaping our designs.

Whereas a linear approach to communication-as-design is built on the expectation that communication always costs time, a nonlinear approach to communication-as-design allows for communication to save time in task completion. A nonlinear approach was key to the success of the authors fellowship I described earlier. No busy person thinks to themselves, "What I really need is another meeting and more work." Yet, writing groups that take time to hold regular meetings and review each other's work are an honored tradition among prolific writers. This nonlinear relationship between time and communication was also a large part of what Kee's computer scientists and administrators hoped to convey to prospective partners and clients: Invest some time to work with us initially, and we'll save you far more time in the future by vastly speeding up and enriching your work.

Nonlinear approaches to time reflect a slow communication design logic. The perception of a strictly linear relationship between time and communication reflects a fast communication design logic. Kee reports that many researchers who would benefit from the use of cyberinfrastructure, and ultimately save time, forego the opportunity because they find it difficult to conceive of adding one more time commitment to their already full schedules.

Although nonlinear trajectories often require more time (i.e., duration) to unfold, this is not always the case. Research shows that up to 90 percent of interactions in organizations occur through *unplanned conversations*—that is, "workplace interactions in which none of the characteristics—the agenda, timing, and participants—is established in advance,"[40] a theoretical concept developed by Dron Mandhana, a communication scholar and frequent collaborator of mine. Unplanned conversations occur outside of scheduled, timed activities such as meetings and take very little time—some research reports it only takes thirty-eight seconds on average.[41]

Additionally, the value of unplanned conversations accrues over time. Any one particular conversation is expendable, but in aggregate, they are crucially important.[42] Mandhana tracked the interaction patterns of several groups of employees across multiple weeks to learn more. His participants reported that these brief interactions led to valuable information needed to do their jobs. Not surprisingly, unplanned conversations occurred less often when members felt pressed for time and participants' interaction norms tended toward a fast communication design logic.[43]

3. What Is the Underlying Belief About What Human Interaction Offers?

Mandhana also found that unplanned conversations occurred more often when members felt safe sharing ideas and asking for advice without fear of reprisal or embarrassment. This reflects a quality of human interaction and relationships that goes beyond a simple transaction between two or more people. Thus, a third element separating fast and slow communication design is an underlying belief about what interaction offers. In the case of fast communication design, interaction is transactional and approached in order to extract particular known resources, such as the expertise of a colleague or the patronage of a client. In figure 1.4, this is depicted by two sequential lines going in different directions—such as a direct question being asked and then answered in response. In contrast, slow communication design is based on an underlying belief that interaction transcends the value of known resources and, instead, makes us collectively available to resources that we cannot anticipate needing until the need appears. The repeated references to trust and relationship building throughout Kee's research on virtual organizing and supercomputing reflect a belief in interaction as transcendent. This is reflected in figure 1.4 by multiple sets of sequential lines that begin with a simple interaction but proceed to give birth to multiple interactions—such as a question and answer—that go far beyond what can be anticipated in a simple transaction. Transcendence requires a willingness to invest in human interaction without an obvious short-term payoff, whereas a belief in relationships as transactional is associated with shortsighted investments.

Attention to temporal processes is key to all three design elements. Whereas transcendent communication refers to the nonlinear process of surpassing and *going beyond* a perceived time limit, a transactional approach to communication is a linear, limited *compromise within* perceived time limits. Underlying beliefs about what interaction offers is tightly interdependent with the previous two elements: the perceived shape of the trajectory between time and communication and the time frames invoked in interaction. Slow communication design supports multiple time frames, a nonlinear trajectory, and is based on an underlying belief that investing in human interaction allows the possibility of transcending time. Fast communication design focuses on singular time frames, a linear trajectory, and an underlying belief that interaction is best approached as a transaction.

As with the previous two elements, transcendence is not reliant upon long stretches of time or even long-standing and intimate relationships. Early work by communication researcher Eric Eisenberg describes the concept of "jamming" in professional settings, defined as "instances of fluid behavioral coordination that occur without detailed knowledge of personality."[44] Jamming occurs through collective action, including in organizational settings. It is similar to the concept of "flow," developed by social psychologist Mihaly Csikszentmihalyi, which is a feeling of such total involvement in an activity that attention to time disappears.[45] However, jamming is a mutual accomplishment that occurs through particular ways of relating to each other as opposed to being an individual, psychological experience as is the case with flow. Transcendence is one of the hallmarks of jamming. Eisenberg explains that in transcendent interaction, "when an individual meets another, he or she directs full attention toward the other, but not necessarily to garner personal knowledge or experience. Instead, the attention is born of a desire to stand in relation to the other, with full respect for his or her individuality."[46]

I collaborated with a former student, Andrew Ishak—a communication researcher who specializes in teams that work in high-pressure, time-sensitive environments such as tactical police units and fire crews—to explore how and why teams in these settings pause in the middle of action to briefly check in about what to do and regroup before moving forward.[47] This is a phase of action called "adaptation." In the midst of an unfolding emergency, adaptation is focused on the task but relies heavily on dynamic communication among team members to quickly discern their best chances for success—for example, realigning with a predetermined strategy or shifting course altogether. Adaptation is highly improvisational in nature and not well suited to a transactional approach in relating to others. Instead, a transcendent approach allows members to step *outside of the time pressure* and meet focused on the moment. In contrast, a transactional view of interaction leaves members *distracted by the time pressure,* and consequently, they miss opportunities for connection and observation that reside in the moment. Based on the research in this area, we argue that this "time-out" period is crucial to a team's success despite the fact that it takes time. Attention to the transcendent nature of interaction reflects a nonlinear trajectory between time and interaction.

Transcendence can also occur outside of severe time pressure and in the context of long-term relationships, as Kee's work suggests. The focus of this communication-as-design element is on the orientation individuals bring with them to each interaction. Notably, the belief about what interaction offers is not a statement of personal ideals or needs. Rather, it is a practical statement that relates directly to accomplishing the task at hand. I observed this firsthand with my family physician. I faced troubling health problems at the time, and initially I saw a lot of different doctors through the "managed care" offered by my health insurance. The communication-as-design of the managed-care visits was strictly transactional—the physicians had just a few minutes to quickly retrieve relevant information in hopes of being able to address my symptoms. Each doctor was constrained by brief appointment times, overbooking, and financial penalties if they did not meet a patient quota set by their medical group. None were able to help me within the constraints they faced, despite their best efforts. Frustrated by appointments that took a lot of logistic time and effort but went nowhere in terms of improving my health, I opted to try a doctor in private practice who approached medicine (and communication-as-design) differently.

Central to the question of what relationships offer, appointments with this new doctor specializing in preventative medicine included detailed discussion of each patient's lifestyle, goals, and daily routine, and they often veered slightly off topic from health complaints as a natural conversation does. Whereas my other doctor's appointments averaged about ten minutes each, this new doctor's annual appointments were about ninety minutes. His medical practice effectively designed time (i.e., the minutes allotted to a given appointment) around temporality (i.e., shared experiences about the general amount of time needed to support communication processes such as information sharing, conversation, and relationship building). The cost was greater because he did not take insurance (hence my early hesitation), but I later realized that the combined cost of the other appointments was equivalent.

My health began to improve after seeing him, but that does not capture the quality of transcendence I want to describe. After all, longer appointment times can also simply capture additional "transactions," thus improving their odds of success. The transcendent communication became obvious years later when, late one night during flu season, my young daughter had a fever that lasted for a couple days and a nasty stomach virus. As background, my doctor invited, all of his patients with young children to call him at any time of the day or night should they have an acute and concerning illness—a common situation for first-time parents. In this instance, I had taken my daughter to her pediatrician a day or two earlier and that night contacted the on-call nurse for help in keeping her fever down. When the nurse told me that I should immediately go to the emergency room (ER) for this modest fever, I was surprised and called my personal doctor for a second opinion. He instructed me to give her a particular dose of ibuprofen and to call him back after a particular period of time. Her fever improved based on his advice, and we got to avoid a trip to the ER in the middle of the night.

Later, when I asked him how he knew that it was unnecessary to take my daughter to the ER, he remarked, "Because I *know* you, and you would have already been at the ER if you had any signs that this was more than a run-of-the-mill stomach bug. You're an incredibly careful, cautious person and you pay attention." He also explained that because the night nurse had no history with me, what she suggested was a perfectly appropriate path to cover all of her bases for all kinds of patients. The nurse had specific information about my daughter's illness but lacked other relevant information that offered context. In contrast, my doctor (who earned an undergraduate degree in art before completing his training as a medical doctor) had designed his private practice with this belief in interaction as transcendent. All of those years in all of the various interactions with me, he was noticing and observing without any real goals other than to understand me. His slow communication design leveraged the transcendence of interaction to enable him to use time and resources more effectively.

Summary

Designs for time are incredibly powerful tools for shaping human interaction. In this chapter, I have illustrated how design is a natural fact about communication and elaborated multiple relationships between time and communication-as-design. After distinguishing between time (which is designed by humans through communication) and temporality (which exists without human intervention), I explored how time can be designed to contain and support temporal processes. Two contrasting communication-as-design strategies employed to manage time-sensitive work demands were then described as fast and slow based on three key elements—the *time frame* of the interaction, the *perceived shape of the trajectory* between time and interaction, and the underlying belief about *what interaction offers.*

The ultimate goal of both fast and slow communication design logics is the same in terms of speed of action. As described, however, each differs in the underlying theory about how communication works to achieve this goal. Slow communication logics focus on how communication can be designed to support temporal processes. Fast communication logics focus on how communication can be designed to take less time. The focus of *Time by Design* is to articulate a set of principles that reflect underlying theories of communication guiding these divergent approaches. As such, it leverages a communication-as-design perspective to offer a transdisciplinary approach to understanding time.

To support that goal, in the following chapter ("Design Frames"), I offer a finer point on the designable features of time, elaborating twelve dimensions of time developed and validated across a range of organizational settings.[48] These dimensions of time are useful in understanding how fast and slow CDLs are about much more than pacing. Each of these dimensions is one among many lenses that organizational members may use as they hypothesize how communication works best and intervene accordingly. These hypotheses are reflected in our enactments, or performances, of time related to *pace, linearity, availability, flexibility, scheduling, punctuality,* and *delay.* These performances are recursively driven by our understanding of time along the dimensions of *urgency, scarcity,* as well as *past, present,* and *future focus.*

2
Design Frames: Communication and the Designable Features of Time

Cinema is a matter of what's in the frame and what's out.

—Martin Scorsese

Our theories of communication lead to different designs for time. In the previous chapter, "Time Talks," I identified three elements that help us distinguish between fast and slow communication design logics:

1. The time frame of the interaction
2. The perceived shape of the trajectory between time and interaction
3. The underlying belief about what interaction offers

Each of these elements reflects an underlying theory about the role of communication in accomplishing time-constrained tasks for a given context or setting. From a slow logic, time should be designed to fit the communication. The temporal process drives the time. From a fast logic, communication should be (re)designed to fit the time. The time drives the quality and quantity of communication. Ultimately, slow logics design time to include the central communication process that defines an event or activity, whereas fast logics design time without regard to the underlying communication process.

In this chapter, we move from these general principles about fast and slow (i.e., the "what") to address exactly how these designs are constructed in our day-to-day lives. If design is a natural fact about communication, as described in chapter 1, this means that we already encounter countless designs in our daily life—from the (nonverbal) message sent by a colleague who looks down at their watch to hurry along a conversation to the formal messages sent by an employer about problems with attendance, attention, or punctuality at video-conferenced meetings. If our communication is always designing time, how does this occur? As elaborated in the following pages, we (purposefully or inadvertently) use the designable features of time to craft our interactions—making particular kinds of communication more likely and making other kinds of communication less likely.

A useful way to think about how these designable features of time come together to produce a fast or slow design logic is through the metaphor of frames and framing.[1] Framing is a core creative tool, as expressed by the celebrated filmmaker Martin Scorsese: Cinema is a matter of what's in the frame and what's out.[2] In cinema, all directors have the same goal—that is, to support the artistry of the cast and crew in a way that leads to a great film—but each has different ideas about how to achieve it. Decisions about framing are what a director brings to the screen. What gets included and excluded in any given moment is what makes, shapes, and shifts the cinematographic experience. Similarly, the difference between fast and slow CDLs begins with what temporal processes are included in the frame. Rather than relying upon varied optical lenses and camera angles to frame a given scene, in the practice of communication-as-design, the *timescale* at which a process is allowed to unfold and the *time dimensions* used (intentionally or unintentionally) to shape a given interaction are the respective framing tools. Together, these designable features of time can be used to intervene in communication to reshape and reform what is possible. Thus, design intervention relies upon carefully assessing three interrelated features of any communication setting:

1. The communication process
2. The timescale of the communication process
3. The time dimensions (assumptions and practices) that support or impede this communication process

Thoughtful attention to each of these features is the foundation of the Chronemic Design Toolkit, elaborated throughout this chapter.

The Designable Features of Time: Timescale and Time Dimensions

Timescale

In chapter 1, I observed that good design takes time. This is because it requires experimenting with varied frames to ensure relevant temporal processes (such as establishing trust, developing rapport, and managing conflict) tied to the communication phenomena of interest (such as effective meetings, productive conversations, or project collaborations) are included. Attention to these temporal processes informs the designer's choice of *timescale* (i.e., a length of time, elaborated below, that can contain or exclude a temporal process). This decision is central to all design efforts because the chosen timescale of a design effort frames the phenomena as we know it. It shapes what *is* as far as we're concerned. It reveals our decision about what matters, driven by our theory about the interrelationships among time, temporality, and communication. To return to Scorsese, the timescale we choose reflects "what's in the frame and what's out." Therefore, its size may need to be iteratively assessed and reassessed to get it right. Eventually, it will be smaller or larger, wider or narrower, zoomed in or zoomed out.

Ida Sabelis, an organizational anthropologist and expert in time studies, argues that both focus and zoom are key tools for understanding and capturing temporal processes.[3] She ponders, "Imagine we are asked to look at the picture of a flower. We cannot know right away if this flower is blooming on a mountain, in a garden or even in a conservatory. We first have to look closely at the picture to find some cues about the (often indistinct) background to the sharply focused center. In order to 'know' about this flower, we have either to 'zoom out' to obtain an impression about its 'context' or we may even 'zoom in' to learn more about its details."[4] Key to her point is that we may not immediately understand our object of interest (i.e., a given temporal process). We won't know if it is constrained and brief or large and expansive. Instead, it takes considering multiple frames of varying sizes before we can fully understand it. The image in figure 2.1 suggests the different things we can know about a phenomenon, depending upon whether we focus in or zoom out. We can get to know quite a lot about this flower by zooming in. For instance, we will learn that it's a daisy. It is white. We can zoom in closer to see the number of petals and other details. But unless we zoom out, we will never know that it is beachside. We will not know what the overhead skies look like. We will not see the mountains behind it.

The definition of timescale offered by management scholars Srilata Zaheer, Stuart Albert, and Akbar Zaheer further illustrates how designs embody hypotheses about, among other things, how long a temporal phenomenon takes to unfold: "By 'time scale' we refer to the size of the temporal intervals, whether subjective or objective, used to build or test theory about a process, pattern, phenomenon, or event."[5] Thus, all design rests upon a working presumption about the timescale of a phenomenon. Based on this

Figure 2.1
The inclusionary and exclusionary qualities of timescale.

presumption, design frames the temporality of that phenomenon—
ultimately, including or excluding aspects of it. Notably, our designs
frequently use intervals that can be referred to objectively (e.g., a
given number of days or years), but even these intervals are derived
through our subjective judgments (e.g., suppositions about how
long a process should take or when it is complete).

We can readily see this intersection of objective and subjective timescales when considering geological timescales—a process
that has received attention recently in the fields of design and
human–computer interaction.[6] Geologists use timescale to distinguish major geological events, beginning with the formation
of Earth's crust. The intervals are, of course, vast—on the scale of
millions of years. Nonetheless, geological timescale illuminates
the objective–subjective distinction especially well. It is objective

in the sense that these events occurred at a particular time in the past. As such, geological timescale uses years to form an account of those various eons, era, periods, and epochs on Earth. However, it is subjective because it took many geologists working across time and through many repeated observations to arrive at a *shared understanding* of the scale of those key events, named for the major geological occurrences during that interval. Further, geological time is an ongoing project of some debate. For example, from 2009 to 2024, the Anthropocene Working Group, made up of various members of the scientific community across disciplines, sought to determine whether we are in a new, distinct geological epoch.[7] In 2024, their proposal to designate a new epoch called the Anthropocene was rejected by the international Subcommission on Quaternary Stratigraphy.[8] Thus, timescale may have an objective referent that we use to describe it, while often being subjectively shaped as well. In the case of geological time, this occurs through trial and error as well as debate across generations of scientists.

In the case of organizational communication, a commonly used timescale is the fiscal year and the variety of reporting requirements tied to it. The fiscal year tends toward the objective side of the continuum because it can be determined by some objective measure (i.e., defined by 365 days). Nonetheless, it still has somewhat subjective origins because not all industries follow the same fiscal year, itself an invention. Agricultural work, in particular, relies largely upon objective intervals (i.e., completely outside of the control of the designer). This includes the measure of a day, the life cycle of crops or animals, and the seasons. However, subjective norms in industrial farming have shifted reliance on certain objective intervals through workarounds such as indoor farming that rely on electric lighting or growth hormones to speed up the life cycle of animals.

In contrast to fiscal years or agricultural seasons, the timescale of some phenomena is principally determined and experienced through a subjective lens. For instance, patrons expect the timescale of a meal at a fine-dining establishment to be longer (e.g., lasting hours) compared to ordering at a drive-through restaurant (e.g., lasting minutes). Rather than getting food quickly (as is the communication design logic of a drive-through, described in chapter 3), patrons of a fine-dining establishment generally expect to dine at a "leisurely" pace. These expectations are expressed using objective intervals but are determined by subjective, institutional norms wherein drive-through restaurants and fine-dining establishments are organized through different CDLs. Additionally, there are individual and cultural levels of subjectivity that shape timescale. For instance, exactly what "leisurely" means in terms of a measurable time interval varies widely across people and cultures.

The role of culture in shaping the timescale of fine dining was highlighted for me when I traveled to the University of Maastricht in the Netherlands for a research symposium. Scholars from across Europe, the United Kingdom, and the United States convened to discuss their research on time and organizational theory.[9] One evening, our wonderful hosts treated us to an exquisite dinner. We talked, laughed, toasted. It was a fantastic event. Eventually, however, the three Americans (me included) started to worry that it would never end. Course after delicious course was being presented, and the final course seemed to be nowhere in sight. At about 11:00 p.m., the three of us huddled and decided that we should discretely excuse ourselves because the meal had gone from "leisurely" to something else altogether. We couldn't blame our decision on jet-lag because one of the Americans lived in Maastricht. It was simply our subjective judgment[10] of the apt timescale for dinner, especially a conference dinner where we had work to do the next morning. Everyone else stayed, while the Americans followed different (and certainly less entertaining) subjective norms.

Thus, the first step in communication-as-design is understanding the timescale for the phenomena of interest in both subjective and objective intervals. As the preceding anecdote shows, the appropriate choice may not be immediately clear or uncomplicated, and it may vary across stakeholders. There may also be ambivalence and even confusion about *which* temporal process matters—in other words, which processes should be included inside the frame and which should be outside. In the case of the agricultural organizations mentioned earlier, for example, a decision must be made about whether elements of the fiscal year (external to temporal processes) or elements of the work (that define the temporal process) set the timescale. One temporal interval may be tied to the quarterly earnings cycle and maintaining investor relationships through various means of communication, such as quarterly earnings reports. Another temporal interval may be tied to the egg-producing cycle of hens owned by a small family farm and maintaining relationships with the stores that will carry these eggs (i.e., one design frame) and the customers who will buy them (i.e., another design frame).

In summary, the chosen timescale of a design effort is centrally important because it shapes what *is* as far as we're concerned. To extend Sabelis's example of using zoom and focus to understand a flower, two criteria are especially helpful to guide decisions about timescale, ultimately landing on a given frame. We can nest these two criteria within the three features of a communication setting that guide this chapter. Put in the form of practical questions, we ask:

- **#1: What is the underlying process?** Organizations operate through multiple communication processes (that include external communication processes such as service delivery and promotion as well as internal communication processes such as professional socialization and rapport among colleagues) each of which demands zoom and focus to fully understand. In Sabelis's analogy, we can think of a flower as the process of interest. Getting to know and understand that flower—what type of flower it is and what stage of growth it is at, for example—requires zooming in and out to better see its various qualities and character. As soon as we know what kind of flower it is, we will already have a better idea of how long it will bloom. In the example of my dinner with colleagues, we can see that identifying the underlying process might be complicated because of subjective norms about what the process "dinner with colleagues" should include or exclude. This is true of all communication processes and leads to the second question.

- #2: **What is the timescale of the communication process?**
  - *What subjective norms are used to define it?* In the case of dinner with colleagues, the answer to this question will vary considerably by culture. This is why we must take various subjective norms into account to understand the timescale of a communication process. For instance, does "dinner with colleagues" include enough time to properly digest a meal and chat briefly with friends? Or is it just enough to satisfy our hunger and then move on to the next task? Is it an opportunity to form new acquaintances and to make important memories with old ones? In Sabelis's analogy, we may discover the flower is a partially opened rose bud, for example. If we want to include it in a floral design, then we will use subjective norms to determine at what stage of growth it should be included. Do we desire a completely opened bud? A fully opened flower? This decision will depend on the intended function. For instance, a fully opened flower may be used in an arrangement that needs to last just one day (e.g., at a wedding) but not for one where the recipient will want to enjoy it for longer (e.g., a birthday gift sent to a friend's home). Therefore, we must decide on the intended function of a given communication process to fully apprehend its timescale.
  - *What is the corresponding objective interval of the process?* The answers to #1 and #2 above point to a given time interval. For the American scholars, dinner with colleagues meant a shorter interval than for the Europeans. Less was intended to occur

(we were mostly focused on the food). So, we didn't need as much time (spent socializing). That is the timescale of Sabelis's flower for our purposes.

- **#3: What time-based dimensions (assumptions and practices) support or impede this communication process?** As the third question suggests, there are additional factors—beyond the zoom and focus—that "frame" a scene. The varied dimensions of time, described next, act as camera lenses, narrowing our attention in particular ways and expanding it in others.

Time Dimensions: Assumptions and Practices That Act as Lenses on Interaction

In addition to the timescale we use to frame phenomena, we also design time through time-based assumptions and practices that help make certain forms of communication possible and help us avoid other forms. For instance, organizations often schedule aspects of the workday in order to make it easier for members to communicate quickly with colleagues. It is certainly possible to coordinate with someone on a different schedule, but asynchronous communication involves delay. Organizational communication is full of these sorts of practical interventions (e.g., scheduling) that reflect underlying assumptions (e.g., urgency). Together, these various *assumptions* and related *practices* reflect our wide-ranging *experience of time* that becomes how we see the world.

I developed and validated a survey instrument to measure each of these twelve dimensions as well as their relationship to each other.[11] The questionnaire has been widely used across contexts as diverse as health care, technology-intensive settings, social services, grief recovery, environmental campaigns, and instructional communication as well as across international settings that extend to Malaysia, Kenya, France, Spain, and Portugal. As described below, it can be used by individuals, teams, and departments to assess their underlying assumptions and shared practices. Figure 2.2 illustrates them as various apertures that frame communication phenomena.

Five assumptions

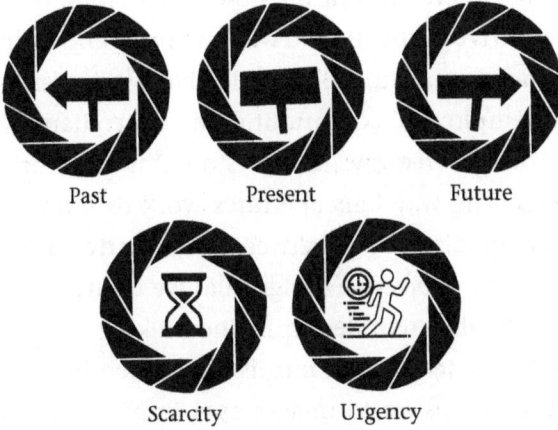

Past

Present

Future

Scarcity

Urgency

Seven practices

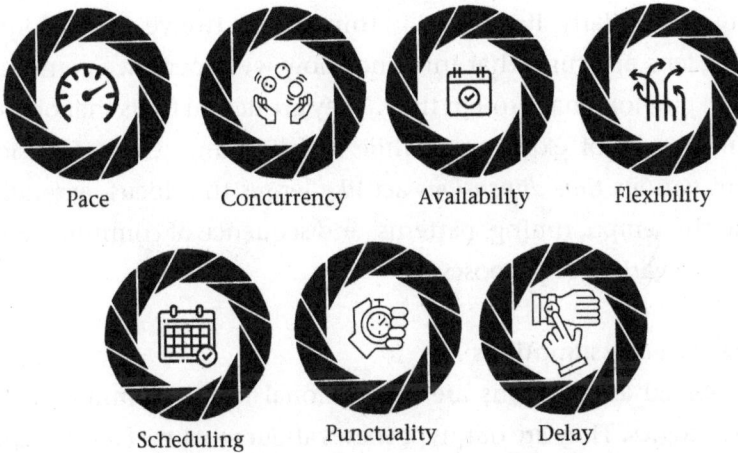

Pace

Concurrency

Availability

Flexibility

Scheduling

Punctuality

Delay

Figure 2.2
Twelve time dimensions: five assumptions and seven practices that act as lenses on interaction.

Rather than merely illuminating some objective time that we encounter "out there" in our day-to-day activities, our experience of time is reflective of the myriad ways we bend and shape time into designs of our own making. This collective "we" refers to the families, friends, employers, communities, and merchants with whom we interact on the freeways, in the stores, at our workplaces, and in our homes. The way lens apertures work to frame a scene also help to make the distinction between an objective reality to which we respond and a subjective design that we create. Our experience of time is that subjective design in the making. An aperture (i.e., an opening in the lens that controls how much light gets into the camera) adds dimension to images as it impacts the exposure (or brightness) and depth of field (or what comes most clearly into focus based on the relationship between the background and foreground). Similarly, it is useful to think of the twelve dimensions as varied lens apertures that influence how we experience communication phenomena through time. They are design tools that obscure some aspects of experience while highlighting others. Decisions about various *time dimensions* act like lenses that focus, extend, or bend the tempo, timing, patterns, and sequence of communication toward a variety of purposes.

Time-Based Assumptions

Time-based assumptions are foundational to our communication design logics. They are our hypotheses about what we face in a communication setting and the best ways to focus our attention. They are accounted for in our appraisal of time's *scarcity* and *urgency*, as well as our *past*, *present*, and *future* time foci.

Scarcity refers to the assumption that there is inadequate time for a given task. At a fundamental level, industrialized work is based on scarcity. It is in the very design. When time became money through industrial capitalism, time assumed all of the same qualities that we typically attribute to money. It became seen as tangible, valuable, and, consequently, scarce. Organizational members may talk about the need to "buy some time" or "save time" at one end of the continuum, or at the opposite end, they may express the need to "spend" or "use up" time if a task or event seems to go on too long. The experience of scarcity directs our thinking, as economist Sendhil Mullainathan and psychologist Eldar Shafir describe how it leads us to make a variety of poor decisions.[12]

Urgency is the assumption that a given task or situation is of pressing importance. This judgment may be independent of some objective measure, as early research on the Type A behavior pattern found. Physicians Ray Rosenman and Meyer Friedman identified an underlying sense of time urgency that people maintained despite external demands, labeled "hurry sickness," as driving individuals' Type A behavior.[13] Despite the lack of substantiation for some of their assertions, the link between time urgency and Type A behavior has been supported across studies and across time. As elaborated in chapter 3, I collaborated with communication scholars Yoram Kalman and Ana Aguilar to study what we call "chronemic urgency," or the urgency users assign to messages received via a specific communication medium.[14] We found that communication norms associated with a given medium (i.e., expectations of a quick response) can be powerful influences on our experience of urgency. In particular, high levels of urgency can be driven by our desire to form good impressions and show positive regard for others. This urgency is by design because it keeps users' attention.[15] At the other end of the continuum, individuals or groups may find that showing regard is best accomplished by minimizing assumptions of urgency.

The three other time-based assumptions concern our relationship to the past, present, and future. Each is a distinct dimension on separate continua, so the focus on any one area does not prevent equal focus on another area. For example, being strongly focused on the past does not preclude also being strongly focused on the future. In fact, according to management scholar Allen Bluedorn's research on temporal depth, or "the combined distance into the past and future that individuals and organizations consider when contemplating events that have happened, may have happened, or may happen," organizations that fail to consider the future also fail to consider the past.[16] He and colleague Stephen Ferris describe this phenomenon using the concept of depth of field found in optics as a metaphor.[17] They observe "the shorter the depth of field, the shorter the distances in front of and behind the object that will be in focus. To follow through on this metaphor, the individual or organization at the present moment would correspond to the object on which the camera is focused, and temporal depth, like depth of field, is the total distance in front (into the future) and behind (into the past) that individuals or organizations typically consider when they think about things that have happened or may happen."[18]

A *past time focus* places the role of tradition—either honoring or avoiding the ways things have always been done (each at opposite ends of the continuum)—as central to ongoing practices. It is designed into awards named after founding members as well as in time-honored traditions that are maintained across decades and centuries. An organization's history often drives assumptions about whether maintaining or escaping a focus on the past is more desirable. It is an issue of perspective. Well-established, successful organizations often valorize their past, whereas newer organizations that see themselves as industry disruptors may position tradition and custom as archaic. To Bluedorn's point, many have critiqued the Silicon Valley culture of disruption as being completely devoid of any sense of future responsibility.[19]

A *future time focus* concerns attention directed toward long-term needs and goals. This assumption can be reflected in many different norms and practices. It can be reflected in a commitment to reducing turnover by investing in people and relationships (inside the organization and with external stakeholders as well). This future focus might also be evidenced in sustainable labor and environmental practices. Nonetheless, industrialized organizations are notoriously lacking in a future focus, given the general focus on scarcity of resources.[20] The guiding hypothesis of many organizations reflects an assumption that—when resources are lacking—a focus on the future is a luxury that one cannot afford. Chapter 4 offers an extended case study that debunks this assumption.

Finally, a *present time focus* centers on the extent to which attention is directed toward events and activities unfolding in the moment. Attention to crises is a typical example of a present time focus. As such, this lens can be used effectively to narrow one's field of vision to avoid overwhelm and focus on the most pressing demands. The challenge, however, especially in turbulent organizational environments where crises are the norm, is to use this approach in conjunction with a past focus and a future focus. Effective teams and organizations will also devote attention to reflection (past focused) and charting a path forward together (future focused). Thus, the present is not at the opposite end of a continuum shared by the future.[21] Instead, both a strong present-time focus and a strong future-time focus are essential to thriving in crisis over the long term.

Time-Based Practices

Whereas time-based assumptions reflect our appraisal of the temporal environment we face, our time-based practices reflect underlying hypotheses about what to do in order to shape and respond to that environment. Practice is used not only in the sense of a noun—as describing particular behaviors—but also in the sense of a verb—as performances that we engage in repeatedly. Hence, our time-based practices include our *pace, concurrency, availability, flexibility, scheduling, punctuality,* and *delay.*

Pace, simply put, refers to the tempo or rate of activity (i.e., the number of inputs per unit of time) and is on a continuum from slow to fast. For instance, organizations may hypothesize that an accelerated work pace is necessary to keep up with the speed of new inputs. In this case, a customer service call that takes less time may be judged as better than a call that takes more time, and their technological infrastructure will likely have design features that monitor employees' speed.[22] Yet, other organizations may hypothesize that establishing a brand for superior customer service (which might sometimes take longer) is the best strategy to manage a crowded market. Zappos famously boasts of a customer-service call that lasted ten hours and forty-three minutes.[23]

Concurrency refers to the number of tasks carried out together (i.e., at a given time). This can range from unitasking (i.e., doing one thing at a time), on one end of the continuum, to multitasking (i.e., attempting to do many things at once), at the other end. Despite the cognitive and behavioral data that demonstrate how multitasking leads to poorer-quality outcomes,[24] many organizations still view it as the sign of a productive employee. It is often designed into work through communication technologies that constantly ping members with notifications about additional tasks to complete.[25]

Availability concerns how we manage distractions or interruptions in the completion of a task. It ranges from making yourself more available to engage with competing demands to the opposite strategy of eliminating distractions by separating ourselves in space or time. Recent technological innovations such as Apple's Focus setting that allows users to make themselves unavailable for any number of reasons (e.g., driving, sleeping, working, and more) and to any number of specific people and audiences is a great example of designing availability. The classic "open door" policy illustrates the spatial element of availability.[26] Although communication technologies make space less important, our use of space remains a powerful messenger in colocated settings. The image of a closed door tells others that we are unavailable to talk, whereas an open door communicates that we are available to interact with others.

Flexibility relates to the degree of rigidity associated with time-based practices. This refers to both daily arrangements such as the timing and length of the workday and a one-off event such as a dental appointment. Can practices and events be easily changed and modified (i.e., flexible), or is this difficult due to logistic or cultural challenges? Some roles are more flexible by design than others. This dimension of time offers a helpful illustration of the relationship between our assumptions and practices. The lenses that we use to frame our world shape and are shaped by basic cultural values. Whereas certain work can be designed as flexible from a logistic and technological point of view, exemplified in pandemic-era work, cultural assumptions about scarcity often make flexible working hours unpopular. Because scarcity offers us the idea of time as a tangible resource, many still expect tangible evidence of time spent working in the form of "face time"[27] during certain hours. In an office setting that values face time, employees who use flexible work arrangements will be evaluated less favorably than others. In contrast with work that doesn't face any logistical or technological challenges, the timing of other work is not flexible because of the level of close coordination needed. For example, the timing with which I hold classes at the university is quite rigid, whereas the timing of my writing is much less so.

The *scheduling* dimension involves the extent to which formal plans are used to structure activities or whether plans unfold more spontaneously.[28] Thus, it is a measure of how formally structured—but not how flexible—plans are. For instance, an event can be both scheduled and flexible. We signify the flexibility of our scheduling by asking others to "pencil in" an appointment or by creating a standing meeting that we routinely decide to forego. Additionally, a schedule can lack flexibility, as in the previous example of when I teach my university class. Instead, if we're focused exclusively on the dimension of scheduling, time can either be tightly scheduled, as in a day full of specific appointments (each with a finite beginning and ending), or loosely scheduled, as in a day's activities based on a to-do list, with no specific boundaries regarding either when something must occur or how much time is allocated to complete it. At the high end of the scheduling continuum, organizational members often need to negotiate regarding whether they can "fit" additional activities into their schedule.

Punctuality concerns whether the timing of activities is more precisely or more loosely determined. In certain industries, it is critical that events are precisely coordinated in order to ensure the safety of work processes. For instance, military time must be precise: "If one GPS satellite is off by a billionth of a second, your GPS receiver will be a foot off. If the satellite's clock were off by one full second, your location on Google Maps would appear to be about two-thirds of the way to the Moon."[29] Accordingly, the United States Naval Observatory has an entire unit called Time Services in the Department of Defense responsible for maintaining time via the Master Clock. Nonetheless, rather than being absolute, punctuality varies across settings. In my field research, I initially hypothesized that time would be either punctual or delayed. But I found that people responded to the idea of punctuality as being in degrees.[30] As an example, although a nation may rely upon a Master Clock to coordinate satellites, people who travel abroad to other countries to work or study soon learn that punctuality exists in gradations. To be punctual to an event in many cultures means showing up within thirty minutes of the formal start time. This is simply less (precisely) punctual, but it is not the same as being delayed—the final time dimension in our design toolkit, discussed next.

Delay refers to a continuum that ranges from maintaining action within preestablished plans to acting outside of those timelines. The example of airline travel is useful for a couple of reasons. We are accustomed to service delays when flying commercial. So, it can easily be characterized as an industry that scores high on this dimension. However, it also helps us to distinguish between punctuality and delay because this industry also demands precise coordination between air traffic control and the flight crew in order to bring the plane safely to its destination. Therefore, although punctuality is concerned with how precise timing is, delay concerns whether the activity extends beyond predetermined boundaries. Similarly, a National Aeronautics and Space Administration (NASA) launch might be delayed, but it will still demand extremely precise coordination. Thus, delay is an independent (i.e., orthogonal) dimension with punctuality. A different, more mundane, example of the difference between these two dimensions includes someone who shows up punctually to a meeting but is working on a long-term project that is delayed several weeks behind schedule.

Individually, each of these twelve dimensions of time acts like a lens that we pick up and put down to design communication, depending upon our read of the organization's setting and participant goals. Collectively, they allow us to put a finer point on the designable features of time so that no two instantiations of fast or slow communication design are identical. Although I use the terms "fast" and "slow" to underscore the distinct communication affordances of any given design logic, time is always multidimensional as this discussion illustrates. As design scholars Larissa Pschetz and Michelle Bastian describe, human interaction and values create a network of temporalities (beyond simple references to speed).[31] These twelve lenses help create that network.

The Timescape of Communication Phenomena

Together, the timescale and time dimensions used to design a given communication phenomenon form what sociologist and social theorist Barbara Adam calls the "timescape"—that is, the interrelationships among the time-bound and temporal elements of a phenomenon.[32] In communication-as-design, the timescape offers a view of the entire communication setting. This includes the actors involved (organizational members, clients, stakeholders, competitors, etc.), their multiple interaction goals and related identities, the communicative act and channel (or means of communication) including the interaction sequences (such as turn taking, delays, and time-based expectations), as well as the historical and cultural era in which they exist. Each of these features of the setting plays a part in the timescape pictured in figure 2.3. Various communication settings and activities have prototypical timescapes. For instance, we often have a culturally specific understanding of the timescape of a movie theater, a school yard, a bank, or a library. Additionally, our theories of communication predictably change as we move from one timescape to another—what is true of communication in one setting is not true in another.

Like landscape design, timescape design involves working with naturally occurring raw material (in this case, the temporality of a

Figure 2.3
The designable features of a timescape.

phenomenon) to suit a practical time-based purpose. The resulting timescape suggests underlying hypotheses about the interrelationship among time, temporality, and communication. This reflects Aakhus's second principle of communication-as-design: Designs are hypotheses.[33] Hypothesis comes from the Greek *hypo* ("under") and *thesis* ("placing"), meaning "foundation, base; hence, base of an argument, supposition" (Oxford English Dictionary). In the case of fast and slow CDLs, our design decisions are hypotheses based on our underlying theory about how time, temporality, and interaction work together to support goal alignment.

Following our theories, we routinely engage in a complex calculus about how much time to devote to communication to accomplish our goals. The results of this calculation will expand or contract the size of our time frame and the interaction it permits, ultimately including or excluding any number of relevant temporal processes. This design decision—not an objective truth—shapes a timescape. We design timescapes, and therefore we can redesign them. The Patient Revolution (PR), elaborated in the following pages, is an example of a long-term organizational effort to redesign the timescape of the health-care industry. Although it is aided by a professional designer, it is illustrative for non-designers as well. Through privileging temporal processes, they are demonstrating how traditional approaches to care can be redesigned.

The Patient Revolution: Health Care Should Feature Unhurried Conversation

We can see how our theories of communication lead to our designs for time as well as how *designs are hypotheses* through exploring the Patient Revolution, a nonprofit organization and movement to redesign the practice of medicine. The cofounder, Dr. Victor Montori, a physician and researcher at the Mayo Clinic, works closely with Maggie Breslin, a designer and researcher who serves as program director at the PR. The cornerstone of their design approach is "careful and kind care" in which the temporal demands of patient care drive the time devoted to it (i.e., a case of using temporality to design time, described in chapter 1). Montori argues that the standard appointment time frames found in industrial health care exclude, or at least make unlikely, key elements of effective clinical practice. He offers voluminous evidence that patient care is hurt by time-based practices and assumptions that exclude a range of human emotion and interaction.[34] Based on the decades he has spent studying this problem in his own work with patients, he advocates for a communication-as-design intervention in modern health care.

I draw attention to his work as an example of communication-as-design for several reasons. First, his use of the descriptor "unhurried" exemplifies the network of temporalities that give rise to fast and slow communication design logics. Second, his depiction of the way health care *should be* illustrates the underlying theories identified in the first chapter and goes further to proffer multiple design hypotheses about how to accomplish it. Third, the numerous examples Montori offers from his work as a clinician help to further elaborate the many designable features of time—in terms of both the timescale and the time dimensions that frame interaction.

Not Fast or Slow, but Unhurried Conversation

Montori chooses the term "unhurried" to problematize conventional (simplistic) understandings of either fast or slow. He explains:

> More time is not always necessary. Many clinicians will testify about a brief phone call in which a simple clarification was helpful for patients to overcome anxiety or to implement a less frustrating self-care routine. Many will also describe a one-hour visit in which, toward the end, a breakthrough took place that set a favorable course of action for months. Just as brevity can be cruel to patients

and clinicians in need of thicker, deeper time, it is also cruel to waste patients' time by being slow and laborious, or by requiring a face-to-face visit when a brief text message exchange would do.[35]

Montori's examples point out that being unhurried does not mean making patients wait for a response. Unhurried is a reference to communication that is responsive to the temporal, not the time, demands of a situation. Meaningful communication can take seconds or hours. As such, it is an exquisite example of effective slow communication design.

I collaborated with Victor and other colleagues [36] to develop a measurement tool that others can use to assess whether a healthcare conversation is unhurried. We define an unhurried conversation as an ongoing, mutual accomplishment between patient and clinician that proceeds through a range of verbal and nonverbal communication practices wherein one or more participants (mutually) regulate the sequence, spacing (temporal and spatial), and speed of interaction to make themselves available to the other and remove or suspend distractions from the environment in order to improve care. We approached the task by identifying a variety of mostly process-based, not time-based, indicators. Specifically, through observing video-recorded clinical encounters, we examined conversations for the interrelationship among ten dimensions of the conversation that allowed clinicians and patients to fully participate in cocreating an unhurried conversation:

- Moderating the pace of spoken language
- Pausing to allow the other person ample time to speak
- Expressing (as opposed to suppressing) emotions
- Displaying open (as opposed to closed) body language
- Establishing rapport through discussion of off-task topics
- Avoiding conversational interruption
- Engaging in shared turn taking

- Using inviting questions to encourage participation
- Triaging (delaying) topics as needed to create adequate time for a central topic
- Minimizing external interruptions

Note that only two indicators qualify as time-based on a superficial level—that is, the pace of spoken language and triaging (delaying) certain topics to another time. However, our fuller description of talking speed points back to whether the pace was appropriate for what they intended to accomplish (i.e., a process measure). Similarly, triaging topics (such as saying "We'll discuss how to better manage certain health conditions during the next visit") can be used both to maintain an unhurried pace of conversation in the current visit as well as to prematurely end it. Consequently, in all cases, our analysis centers on whether the encounter is based on *time* or on *process*. An unhurried conversation is distinguished from others by making time for what the process demands.

Underlying Theories of Communication

The design intervention proposed by the Patient Revolution highlights the three elements that distinguish a fast versus slow CDL, revealing lay theories about how communication works best in a given timescape. For instance, concerning the *underlying belief about what interaction offers*, Montori describes the prevailing CDL in managed care as reflecting a belief that interaction should be a simple transaction: an exchange of money for access to medical treatment. In contrast to the dominant conception, the design imperative of the PR movement is to end practices that treat health care as a commodity to be exchanged in a simple transaction. Montori elaborates:

> Industrial healthcare fails to notice patients. It standardizes practices for *patients like this*, rather than caring for *this patient* . . . Rigid protocols and fear of deviating from them miss the person. Systems

that prioritize access and volume place very little value on the length and depth of the interaction between patients and clinicians. Forcing encounters to be brief and shallow speeds patients through consultations in which clinicians cannot appreciate patients' situation fully. Failure to notice is also the effect of encounters bloated with industrial agendas, such as documentation and billing, which draw attention away from patients and toward the computer monitor, distracting from care to document it.[37]

He goes on to point out the harm done to clinicians because of this transactional design, referencing the high rates of burnout, divorce, and suicide among doctors—higher per capita than any other profession. Thus, this transactional approach leaves the clinician starved of genuine human connection—ostensibly the reason many entered the field of medicine.

Further, with regard to the *time frame of interaction*, unhurried conversation allows for the physician and patient to explicitly discuss the past, present, and future as it relates to the health challenge with which they are presented. For example, the Patient Revolution offers tools to improve outcomes through supporting unhurried conversation. One tool, a set of notecards called "Tell Us About Your Life," asks the patient to answer four questions prior to a visit with their doctor. The first question asks the patient to name one *nonmedical* thing about their life that they think the doctor should know (e.g., where they grew up). This question immediately signals the relevance of the past to their conversation. Another question asks where the patient finds the most joy in their life. This helps to situate the conversation in both the present (as it concerns the patient's current ability to participate in these activities) as well as the future (as a way of identifying activities the patient would like to resume as their health improves).

As concerns the *perceived shape of the trajectory between time and interaction*, the design and practice of unhurried conversation proceeds from an underlying theory that communication focused on improving patient outcomes is often nonlinear. Montori contrasts linear and nonlinear times that unfold in different places and moments at the clinic:

> At the reception desk and in the waiting room, time keeps flowing forward, relentless as usual. But in some of my encounters, time flows differently. This happens more commonly when patients and I share stories about the sweet and funny within the mundane and trivial; laugh, cry, and relate to each other's events; build grand theories of the world; discover common fears and common tastes. When we are together, it is as if new laws of physics apply.
>
> In these moments, the experience somehow uncouples from the time it should take to have it. Instead of moving forward, time grows denser. In the thick of it, patient and clinician notice each other, and at the right time, the possibilities of care emerge. There is a certain timelessness to care.[38]

This example offers insight both into the nonlinear relationship between time and interaction and into the way transcendent communication unfolds—outside of the quantitative experience of an appointment time yet logistically contained by it. He describes a nonlinear relationship to time, a qualitative feeling of timelessness, that ultimately affords a transcendent communication experience. Montori's description also maps perfectly on to the differences between time (i.e., at the reception desk and waiting room) and temporality (i.e., the process of relating to one another during the appointment).

Aakhus elaborates on the distinction between communication-as-design and other more superficial interventions: "Where other approaches to communication focus on the behavior that occurs within a communication format, design focuses on what those formats presuppose about communication and with what consequence the new format is taken up in communicative practice."[39] Accordingly, Montori does not lead the call to change by asking *only* that clinicians adopt new practices, thus leaving the burden on clinicians to single-handedly transform health care. Instead, he questions the limits of extant health-care design, offering insight into how the time-based norms and procedures in clinical settings frame (and exclude) possibilities for human interaction. This is critical because recognizing the power of particular design features or formats to enable, or completely exclude, interaction is central to communication-as-design work. Below, I elaborate on the designable features of time—the timescale and time dimensions—central to an unhurried conversation.

Designs as Hypotheses: Shaping the Designable Features of Time
Timescale The timescale of unhurried conversations is subjectively determined and will vary based on the particulars of the clinical encounter. Returning to our discussion of timescape, the particulars include the people involved, their multiple interaction goals (Is this a routine checkup or in response to a new illness? Is this a new patient visit?) and related identities (Is this a generally healthy person or a person with a debilitating chronic illness?), the communicative act and channel of communication (Is this a telemedicine visit? Is there a great deal of information that needs to be conveyed?), the interaction sequences (Are they interrupted? Do they establish rapport?), and the historical and cultural era in which they exist (Were effective treatments for the illness available at the time?). Thus, through repeated observations, the Patient Revolution can determine the upper and lower limits of the range of times it takes for an unhurried conversation in the medical setting. Knowing this range improves their ability to design for it.

Note that a subjective timescale does not mean that people cannot agree on it or that it cannot be determined at all. On the contrary, in my earlier example about fine dining with European and American colleagues in the Netherlands, the agreement fell squarely along cultural lines. Although the subjective qualities of culture determined the timescale in that case, in unhurried conversations, the timescale is driven by subjective qualities of human interaction. This subjectivity is inherent to all communication processes. Conversations are, by definition, improvisational. They are a shared accomplishment, an intricate system of dynamic turn taking between two people. Therefore, our understanding of the timescale emerges from what unfolds *during* the interaction, not prior to it. We can later account for this timescale using objective units of time, but we measure it through a shared understanding of its temporal features. For instance, a team of psychologists found that without any other contextual cues, people can reliably judge whether others are connecting or "clicking" simply by viewing a ten-minute conversation between strangers.[40] Their judgments were predicted by the timescale of the turn taking of those conversing (i.e., how quickly they responded to the other, measured in milliseconds). This timescale is so small as to be outside of conscious awareness, suggesting that we draw on tacit knowledge in judging the suitable timescale of an interaction sequence.

There is another note of import concerning timescale: The timescale of a phenomenon's existence (at one moment in time) is distinct from its relationship to other processes. Montori makes this point of clinical care: "That the apparent efficiencies gained by overclocking the doctor will later create waste escapes scrutiny. . . . If the patient situation has now worsened, this may require more aggressive or specialized testing and treatment. The push for more and briefer visits may result in efficiency without effectiveness."[41] Therefore, when viewed comparably with a hurried visit, the longer timescale of an unhurried visit may lead to less time overall due to its effectiveness in the early stages of a treatable illness. As discussed in chapter 1, fast communication design logics are often cumbersome in practice and, ultimately, take more time than slow communication design. That is, even though the existence of a phenomenon (i.e., an unhurried conversation) unfolds in a longer timescale, it can still minimize the overall time spent compared with a phenomenon (i.e., a hurried conversation) that initially unfolds in a shorter timescale.

Time dimensions *Why We Revolt* contains vivid images of the timescape of industrial health care as well as the alternative being designed through the Patient Revolution. It depicts a range of time dimensions that can act like lenses and refract or obscure communication between clinician and patient. Here, I describe the twelve dimensions and related examples that Montori offers.

- The PR advocates that health care remove distractions and offer greater *availability*:

    "We must engineer how to save time for care by peeling away all the commotions that distract, automatizing and removing from the foreground subordinate activities that belong silently in the background."[42]

- Improved scheduling practices will reduce the *concurrent* execution of activities in a way that limits care:

    "Innovations that add fluidity and forgiveness to the schedule may offer new ways for patients and clinicians to collaborate and reduce clinician multitasking."[43]

- Getting care to patients in a time-sensitive, *punctual* manner must remain central to the mission:

    "I recognize that it is hard to get both timely access to care and high-quality care. But we must try . . . In improving efficiency, however, we must respect time for care: A minute is not a minute is not a minute."[44]

- The lens of the patient's life (i.e., their *past*, *present*, and *future*) should always be kept in the foreground:

    "In [patient] lives, a more important and fundamental saga awaits to play out: the pursuit of their hopes and dreams amidst disappointment and misfortune."[45]

- In order to accomplish these goals, the default lens of *scarcity* that currently shapes interactions in health care must be reexamined:

    "Time is not money. The depths of time are the currency for caring."[46]

- Constant *urgency* and busyness hurt not only clinical encounters but also the clinicians:

  "The No. 1 concern clinicians raise is the brevity of the clinical encounter, the busyness of their schedule."[47]
- Current *scheduling* practices fail to achieve careful and kind care because the clinical encounter itself is not centered:

  "There is an equation that sets the duration of the encounter based on how many patients demand care, how many clinicians are available to care for them, and how many minutes are in a workday . . . subordinating the length of the clinical encounter to these goals."[48]
- Designs that create greater *flexibility* in scheduling practices are needed:

  "Far from responding to the demands of care, rigid time schedules stand as evidence of the fictitious equivalence of minutes."[49]
- Simply accepting routine *delays* that result from a poorly designed system is not the solution either:

  "The satisfaction of caring well will face the disappointment of the next patient who is now sick of waiting, and the anger of the clinic staff who, thanks to the 'slow clinician,' will now be late for dinner."[50]
- We have traditionally expected clinicians to pick up the *pace* to accommodate a poorly designed system, and the mission of the PR is to design care around patient needs:

  "Rushing—doing a lot in little time—can 'deliver care' in little time, a favourable productivity statistic of no value to the patient or the clinician if this care is ineffective. The efficient clinic is elegant, not cheap."[51]

The lenses that we use are influenced by culture, and as such, shifting from one to another may present difficulties associated with challenging cultural norms. Thus, Montori concludes *Why We Revolt* by comparing the work of changing industrial health care to building cathedrals—an analogy that reflects how certain objects, practices, or (in this case) institutions are built across generations. The commitment to the work extends beyond one lifetime. Designing "careful and kind care" may not occur easily or quickly, but this is no reason not to begin. The case study of the children's advocacy center (CAC) movement in chapter 4 has similarly been a long-term design challenge, but it has realized many intermediary achievements along the way.

The Chronemic Design Toolkit: Time by Communication-as-Design

In summary, time unfolds in communication-as-design through the timescale and time dimensions used to frame a given communication phenomenon. This iterative design process (depicted in figure 2.4) involves asking a series of questions that allow us to move from the underlying theories of communication that distinguish between fast and slow design logics to the more specific questions of zoom and focus that help us effectively frame (or identify) the temporal and communication demands of a setting. Rather than being determined a priori by the designer, as the preceding discussion illustrates, understanding the latter two features—scale and dimension—emerges through the questions we ask as we engage with the timescape.

I emphasize the processual (i.e., temporal) nature of chronemic design for two reasons. First, the answers to key questions may evolve even after you feel you've reached certainty about the phenomenon, its timescale, or its relevant time dimensions because we can only fully apprehend a process over time. For example, in the first year of joining a new organization, you might initially think you understand the pace of work it demands by your third month. However, as the next quarter in the fiscal year unfolds, you might find that your third and eleventh months are radically different.

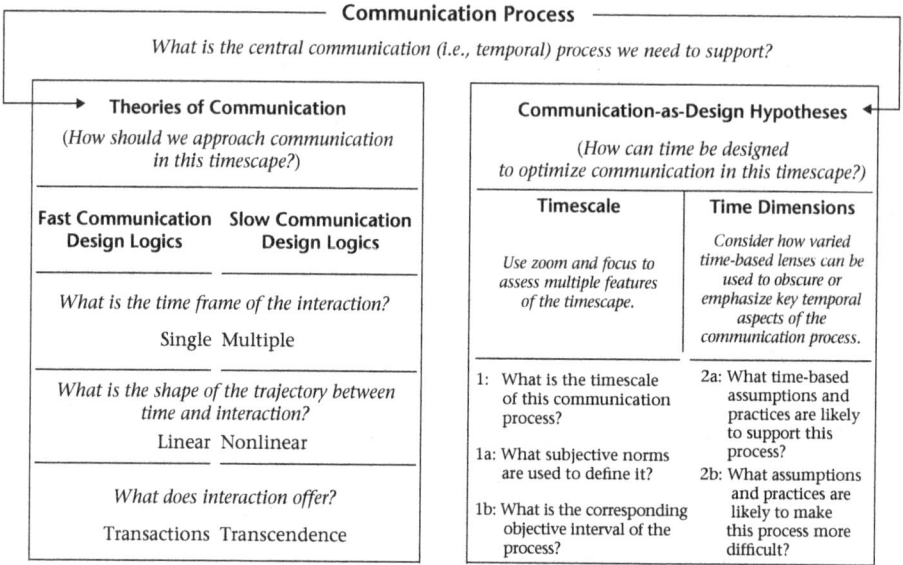

```
┌──────────────────────── Communication Process ───────────────────────┐
│       What is the central communication (i.e., temporal) process we need to support?       │
│                                                                                              │
│  ┌───────────────────────────────┐   ┌─────────────────────────────────┐                   │
│  │ →  Theories of Communication  │   │  Communication-as-Design Hypotheses ◄ │               │
│  │  (How should we approach communication │ (How can time be designed          │               │
│  │      in this timescape?)      │   │ to optimize communication in this timescape?) │        │
│  └───────────────────────────────┘   └─────────────────────────────────┘                   │
└──────────────────────────────────────────────────────────────────────────┘
```

Theories of Communication	Communication-as-Design Hypotheses
(How should we approach communication in this timescape?)	(How can time be designed to optimize communication in this timescape?)

Fast Communication Design Logics	**Slow Communication Design Logics**	**Timescale**	**Time Dimensions**
		Use zoom and focus to assess multiple features of the timescape.	*Consider how varied time-based lenses can be used to obscure or emphasize key temporal aspects of the communication process.*
What is the time frame of the interaction?			
Single	Multiple		
What is the shape of the trajectory between time and interaction?		1: What is the timescale of this communication process?	2a: What time-based assumptions and practices are likely to support this process?
Linear	Nonlinear	1a: What subjective norms are used to define it?	2b: What assumptions and practices are likely to make this process more difficult?
What does interaction offer?		1b: What is the corresponding objective interval of the process?	
Transactions	Transcendence		

Figure 2.4
The Chronemic Design Toolkit: a multi-space process for time by communication-as-design.

In reality, you won't understand the pace of work until a full year of ordinary, mundane work has occurred. Even then, what if, during the twelfth month, the ordinary and mundane disappears as a merger, takeover, or global health pandemic begins? It turns out that social processes are always evolving and simply don't allow for complete certainty. Striving for relative certainty is a far superior approach because *precision* (i.e., knowing exact answers) is less important than *inclusion* (i.e., being sensitive to plausible answers) in chronemic design.

Designers Harold G. Nelson and Erik Stolterman's description of *interpretation*[52] helps explain why complete certainty (regardless of whether it is possible) is not the goal of design. They explicate:

> Interpretation is a subjective process. Interpretation, as a part of the design process, serves the same purpose as evidence and proof do in science[53]. . . . In design, interpretation is not about determining

a solution by closely and objectively analyzing reality in order to
be informed of what action to take. . . . Interpretation in design is
not a search for the objective, true, and precise design imperatives,
hidden somewhere in the richness of reality waiting to be observed.
Instead, design interpretation is an act of judgment. . . . This does
not mean that an understanding of reality based on scientific
methods is useless or misguided. Rather, we would like to bring
scientific decision making and judgment together in a way that is
guided by intention and is holistic in its approach.[54]

Therefore, the hypothetical scenario above where you need to make
an appraisal of the pace of work—perhaps to decide whether to stay
or take advantage of another job offer—demands qualitative *interpretation*, not merely quantitative observation and measurement.
An inclusive answer (i.e., interpretation) about the pace of work in
your new job, then, will take into account the full eleven months,
but it will also include knowledge of industry-wide norms you
gained through chance comparisons with colleagues at other
organizations and things you heard during your first internship in
that field.

The second reason I emphasize that this is a process is because it
also highlights the need for attention to temporality as the designer.
I mentioned this in chapter 1 and further elaborate this point in
chapter 6, but I want to underscore here that chronemic design
takes time. Understanding these design features requires a thoughtful interpretation of the setting through multiple, interrelated questions that guided this chapter. I use the term "multi-space" instead
of "multistep" to reference the three spaces of innovation that the
chief executive officer and president of IDEO, Tim Brown, identifies.[55] He explains:

There are useful starting points and helpful landmarks along the
way, but the continuum of innovation is best thought of as a system
of overlapping spaces rather than a sequence of orderly steps.
We can think of them as *inspiration*, the problem or opportunity
that motivates the search for solutions; *ideation*, the process of

generating, developing, and testing ideas; and, *implementation,* the path that leads from the project room to the market. Projects may loop back through these spaces more than once as the team refines it ideas and explores new directions.

In short, understanding these design features may be an iterative process of trial and error, in the same way that formal hypotheses support theory building. Therefore, Brown recommends prototyping—that is, iteratively trying something out through building it, for faster, better design outcomes. Much like my description of slow communication design logics, he describes it as an instance of going slow to go fast. Prototyping allows a designer to occupy all three spaces of innovation simultaneously.

In chapter 1, I attended to the space of inspiration. It begins with facing a chronemic challenge: *How should we approach communication in this timescape?* Here, in chapter 2, I offered tools to support the space of ideation through identifying the *three key features of a timescape* summarized above and elaborated throughout this chapter. In particular, the designable features of time—its scale and dimensions as applied in a given communication setting—bring either a fast or a slow CDL into full view. Although these tools help to direct the design process, multiple time-based configurations exist across industries and contexts. Next, in chapter 3, I begin to address the space of implementation. Across three case studies, I identify potential realities of communication-as-design in the wild: inconsistent theories of communication, competing theories of communication, and complementary theories of communication. In the case of inconsistent theories, I also explore a potential redesign based on both the field data and related research.

3
Fast Logics: The Communication Theory of More-Faster-Better

Move fast and break things.
   Unless you are breaking stuff, you are not moving fast enough.

                                                                    —Mark Zuckerberg

The designable features of time that we use to shape our work reflect multiple hypotheses about the interrelationship among time, temporality, and communication. Together, in a given configuration, they tell of our grand theory about the best way to get things done. Zuckerberg's infamous slogan—advising his employees to "Move fast and break things. Unless you are breaking stuff, you are not moving fast enough"[1]—is an example of one such theory. It is grounded in fast communication design logics—useful for particular kinds of work and disastrous for other kinds of work (depending on what stuff you are breaking), as I discuss in this chapter.

   In chapters 1 and 2, I offered new design tools and theory that illustrate a key insight I elaborate further here in chapter 3 and, next, in chapter 4: Speed in organizing is never just a time-based issue. The genesis of speed lies at the intersection of time and communication (i.e., chronemics). Although organizational theory has relied almost exclusively on time-based interventions to speed work along since the beginning of industry, that approach is reductive[2] and only works over brief timescales (if even then).[3] *Time by Design*, however, is about the insights that accrue from also considering communication (i.e., taking a chronemic perspective) to illuminate and alleviate problems related to collective action. Accordingly, in this chapter, I apply this perspective across three case studies. In addition to each case study being focused on a distinct communication phenomenon and setting, each demonstrates three important takeaways about the practical reality of implementation. Prior to elaborating the three cases, I briefly describe when fast CDLs came to rise and consider what they mean for relationships in the context of task accomplishment.

The Industrial Origin Story of Fast Communication Design Logics

Recall that the aim of both fast and slow communication design logics is identical: to respond effectively and efficiently to time demands as they arise. However, within each logic, communication functions differently to achieve this outcome. From a fast CDL, communication is simply a way of transmitting information. In this design, more communication always entails more time and is seen as a wasteful luxury. It saves time by not spending it. From a slow CDL, time spent communicating is seen as a valuable investment that builds capacity to respond quickly now and in the future. It saves time through the return on investment it yields. These competing designs simply reflect different underlying theories of communication.[4]

Fast theories of communication pervade contemporary, postindustrial organizations. As described in chapter 1, these theories are part of what we call the classical school of management that was born in the late nineteenth and early twentieth centuries. Despite the origins of this school of thought in shaping factory work and assembly-line processes, it still dominates conventional management thinking in the twenty-first century. As an answer to the problem of speed, fast CDLs are not incorrect. The challenge for a given relationship (whether personal or professional) or organization arises when fast logics are the *only* design for communication. They are appropriate for some limited contexts and roles, but they were not designed to support the whole of contemporary organizing where communication (internal and external) drives the work. They ultimately degrade the relationships upon which we rely in our personal and professional lives.

For instance, the Great Resignation[5] that began in 2021 was driven by the failure of fast communication design logics to deliver working conditions that employees find acceptable. In a Pew Research Center poll, communication (in this case, feeling disrespected at work) ranked among the top three reasons (alongside low wages and the lack of advancement opportunities) people cited as reasons for quitting their jobs. Additionally, problems with time, including lack of flexibility and overwork, ranked among the top ten reasons they resigned.

In light of these cited employee concerns in contemporary work, consider Frederick Taylor's time-and-motion studies that are foundational to the classical school of management[6] that drove the Industrial Revolution. In his book *Scientific Management*, Taylor describes a conversation he held with Schmidt, an employee who was quite good at his job. Taylor wanted to observe and codify Schmidt's processes. He included the following transcript as a "how to" for time-and-motion studies:

T: Schmidt, are you a high-priced man?

S: Well, I don't know vat you mean.

T: Oh yes, you do. What I want to know is whether you are a high-priced man or not.

S: Well, I don't know vat you mean.

T: Oh, come now, you answer my questions. What I want to find out is whether you are a high-priced man or one of those cheap fellows here. What I want to find out is whether you want to earn $1.85 a day or whether you are satisfied with $1.15, just the same as all those cheap fellows are getting.

S: Did I vant $1.85 a day? Vas dot a high-priced man? Vell, yes I was a high-priced man.

T: Oh you're aggravating me. Of course you want $1.85 a day—every one wants it! You know perfectly well that has very little to do with your being a high-priced man. For goodness' sake answer my questions, and don't waste any more of my time. Now come over here. You see that pile of pig iron?

S: Yes.

T: You see that car?

S: Yes.

T: Well, if you are a high-priced man, you will load that pig iron on that car tomorrow for $1.85. Now do wake up and answer my question. Tell me whether you are a high-priced man or not.

S: Vell—did I got $1.85 for loading dot pig iron on dot car tomorrow?

T: Yes, of course you do, and you get $1.85 for loading a pile like that every day right through the year. That is what a high-priced man does, and you know it just as well as I do.

S: Vell, dot's all right. I could load dot pig iron on the car tomorrow for $1.85, and I get it every day, don't I?

T: Certainly you do—certainly you do.

S: Vell, den, I vas a high-priced man.

T: Now, hold on, hold on. You know just as well as I do that a high-priced man has to do exactly as he's told from the morning till night. You have seen this man here (the supervisor) before, haven't you?

S: No, I never saw him.

T: Well, if you're a high-priced man, you will do exactly as this man tells you tomorrow, from morning till night. When he tells you to pick up a pig and walk, you pick it up and you walk, and when he tells you to sit down and rest, you sit down. You do that right straight through the day. And what's more, no back talk. Now a high-priced man does just what he is told to do, and no back talk. Do you understand that? When this man tells you to walk, you walk; when he tells you to sit down, you sit down, and you don't talk back at him. Now you come on to work here tomorrow morning and I'll know before night whether you really are a high-priced man or not.

The tone of this conversation is likely startling. However, I include it for two reasons. First, it is important to understand the prevailing workplace norms when fast communication design logics found their way into industrial organizations.[7] Not only was the idea of building relationships among members of an organization missing, it was also actively discouraged. Second, if you look beyond the tone, the same three elements of fast communication design are evident: transactional relationships ("What I want to find out is whether you want to earn $1.85 a day or whether you are satisfied with $1.15"), linear trajectories ("For goodness' sake answer my questions, and don't waste any more of my time"), and a single frame of interaction ("Now you come on to work here tomorrow morning and I'll know before night whether you really are a high-priced man or not"). While fast CDL may look different in contemporary work, workplace interactions like these were key to its industrial origin story.

In the remainder of the chapter, I present three case studies of how fast communication design logic operates in practice. This includes two examples of when it is misused (because this is most common) and one example of where fast CDL thrives. The first case is extended because it features an especially useful data-collection method to assess fast and slow CDLs within organizational contexts, and it offers a reprise on how the same dynamics can be redesigned to support slow CDLs. Notably, each case points to a unique observation about the reality of communication-as-design implemented in practice. Awareness of how fast CDLs may appear in the wild can be helpful when different stakeholders share conflicting accounts or multiple observations suggest different realities.

1. *Organizations may be inconsistent in what they describe and what they do.* The chronemic theory that organizations publicly declare (i.e., the formal one) and the one that actually guides their work (i.e., the informal one) may not be the same. The Safety Net Healthcare case in this chapter elaborates this inconsistency.

2. *Organizations often have competing chronemic designs.* What members are asked to do may be in conflict with their personal well-being or that of others. In these instances, the organizations' declared and actual chronemic theories may compete for adherents. The American Football case study in this chapter offers an example of this competition.

3. *Fast and slow chronemic designs are naturally complementary, each supporting the other.* The everyday digital communication case study shows how fast communication design logics can be used to complement and support slow CDL.

Each of the following three sections (i.e., inconsistent, competing, and complementary cases) begins with an overview of the timescape and the methods used in the study. This is followed by a description of the key timescape features: the communication process, its timescale, and the central time dimensions (assumptions and practices). In discussing the communication process, I also highlight the underlying theories of communication in that setting through the messages we heard in the field about how best to achieve it. Following the analysis, I offer a snapshot of the CDLs at work using the three elements that distinguish fast and slow CDL. I then conclude with a reflection on the utility of the CDL for that timescape. In the case of Safety Net Healthcare, I offer a reprise to reimagine how the timescape might be redesigned through listening to the insights shared by organizational members.

Table 3.1 compares and contrasts the three case studies along multiple elements of a given communication setting. This includes: the reality of design in the wild that it depicts; the key features[8] of each timescape; and the underlying theories of communication reflected in the timescape. I include it below as an overview or guide for those who find it helpful, or you can use it as a summative chart to be consulted at the conclusion of the chapter.

Inconsistent Theories in the Safety Net Healthcare Timescape: Health Care Versus Triage

Organizations often aspire to ideals that they do not meet[9] and, notably, are not designed to meet. One of the places we can readily see this is when an organization advertises an experience to external stakeholders (e.g., customers) that internal stakeholders (e.g., employees) are not given the resources to deliver. Organizations generally guarantee temporally driven service delivery that will fulfill customers' every need while designing employees' work based solely on time. This leads to *inconsistent theories of communication*, or slippage between a declared theory and how things actually operate. In these cases, only one set of values is acknowledged explicitly. The other (implicit) theory of communication goes unacknowledged, despite everyone knowing it is the truth about how things operate. Put differently, the theory behind mission and vision statements

Table 3.1
Fast communication design logics in the wild

	Safety Net Healthcare	American Football	Everyday Digital Communication
3 Realities of design implementation	Inconsistent theories *Declared theory:* Provide comprehensive, time-sensitive health care (i.e., *whole-person health care*) *Actual theory:* Keep the line moving no matter what (i.e., *triage health care*)	Competing theories *Dominant theory:* Leave it all out on the field (i.e., *short-term plays*) *Competing theory:* Plan for a career on and off of the field (i.e., *long-term goals*)	Complementary theories *Fast theory:* Being available for urgent messages is important *Slow theory:* Delays can lead to forgetting or signal a lack of interest and harm relationships
3 Chronemic Design Features			
1: Communication process	Patient care	Professional socialization	Responsiveness
2: Timescale 2a: Subjective Norms	*Declared:* whole-person health care *Actual:* triage health care	*Dominant:* short-term plays *Competing:* long-term career goals	Immediate to prompt
2b: Objective Interval	*Declared:* whatever it takes *Actual:* minutes	*Dominant:* minutes to hours *Competing:* years to decades	Immediate responsiveness can mean seconds to minutes; prompt responsiveness can mean hours or days
3: Focal time lens(es)	Scarcity and flexibility	Present and future	Urgency and delay

3 Underlying Theories of Communication (Elements of the Communication Design Logic)

1: Time frame of interaction	*Whole-person health care:* past, present, future *Triage health care:* present	*Dominant:* present *Competing:* past, present, future	*Fast logic:* present *Slow logic:* past, present, future
2: Shape of trajectory between time and interaction	*Whole-person health care:* nonlinear *Triage health care:* linear	*Dominant:* linear *Competing:* nonlinear	*Fast logic:* linear *Slow logic:* nonlinear
3: Belief about what interaction offers	*Whole-person health care:* transcendent *Triage health care:* transactional	*Dominant:* transactional *Competing:* transcendent	*Fast logic:* transactional *Slow logic:* transcendent

The Safety Net Healthcare Timescape

Patient care

Scarcity   Flexibility

Triage care   Whole-person care

Inconsistent chronemic theories

Figure 3.1
The Safety Net Healthcare timescape.

that organizations publicly proclaim may not be the same theory around which work is designed in practice.

Therefore, to properly identify the guiding chronemic theory of an organization, both public-facing language (such as that found on company websites and in employee manuals and training) and day-to-day practices must be examined. The processes I observed at Safety Net Healthcare, a pseudonym for a health clinic I studied with a team of colleagues, illustrates how inconsistent theories of communication impact both internal and external members. This inconsistency leads to problems in morale that may shape turnover, and fundamentally, it prevents the organization from achieving its primary mission.

Inconsistent theories may occur despite an organization's best intentions. For instance, they may find themselves facing inadequate resources to meet the virtues they nonetheless hope to deliver to external stakeholders. Alternatively, the inconsistencies may be a deliberate attempt at "bait and switch." In any event, my point here is that when assessing the underlying chronemic theory, one must always look to the norms and routines (i.e., the day-to-day practices) that characterize members' behavior rather than only what organizations formally describe. I underscore norms and routines here because of the need for repeated observations in order to draw a conclusion. If you are looking to assess an organization's timescape (either as a member of that organization or as a designer or other practitioner), bear in mind that they may be undergoing change and working toward greater ideals. Similarly, if you are the person in your organization responsible for leading the change effort and looking to assess its success, it is important to observe whether members' daily practices reflect the intended design. Assessment must go beyond questionnaires and even interviews that only represent what people say—it is important to see what people do. For this reason, in order to illustrate how the formal and informal theories may differ, in this first case, I will describe the methods we used in a bit more detail.

Data Collection: Learning About Communication-as-Design at Safety Net Healthcare

As background, the genesis of this research came from a conversation I held with Dr. Urmimala Sarkar, professor of medicine at the University of California San Francisco. She invited me to campus to talk about my research and, at some point during our conversation between events, I asked about a typical day for her as a physician who sees patients in the clinic, does research, and teaches. The conversation turned to scheduling, and she qualified her answer as based on what she called the "fictive schedule." She went on to point out that this fictive schedule is some approximation of where her time actually goes but that its accuracy ebbs and flows, depending upon the day. It was not a reliable measure of her time as much as it was a formal organizational plan to offer some structure to the various tasks of the day. In terms of these scheduling norms, she talked about the challenges for her patients (i.e., in getting the care they need and organizing their day around traveling to appointments including taking time off of work) as well as herself and fellow colleagues (i.e., in terms of the stress of staying on time while providing needed care) in estimating how long an appointment will take. I was riveted by her account, and we soon realized that this was a health-care challenge we needed to study.

Therefore, from early 2019 until February 2020, when the COVID-19 global health pandemic emerged, our research team[10] observed primary care physicians and their interaction (with the patients' medical teams, patients themselves, and related health-care agencies) to better understand the chronemic design of their work. Locally, in Austin, we studied a medical clinic that serves the needs of underserved health-care populations, part of the national safety net system[11] in the US. Through our fieldwork, we created a system of "time shadowing" to systematically capture and record how physicians spend their time and the nature of their interaction with others. We then shadowed nine different physicians at least twice each, to help us avoid forming conclusions based solely on unusual or atypical days, for a total of eighty-four hours of observation by four different researchers, resulting in seventy-one pages of observation notes. The study concluded in late 2021 with seven in-depth interviews that allowed us to follow up with the physicians we shadowed and to get their reflections as well.

The shadowing process involved four parts. First, throughout a full shift (averaging five hours), we recorded each physician's time spent in various locations (e.g., patient rooms, at their desk charting, talking to medical assistants, etc.). Because of the challenges in capturing such information in a physically dynamic environment where individuals were constantly moving, we typically had two to three team members on site observing the same setting for reliability (as well as practical needs such as bathroom breaks).

Second, we compared these time observations to their *fictive schedule*—that is, the official schedule as determined by the clinic management. From these activities, we gained insight into the differences between their formal schedule and the work they actually performed. We stayed with each physician until the end of their shift, that often extended beyond the scheduled time.

A third aspect of time shadowing included taking ethnographic notes based on salient observations throughout the shift. Depending upon the pace of work or unusual events, sometimes we held conversations with physicians and their team during their shift, including interns, medical assistants, nurses, administrators and social workers, to understand more about what we were observing.

A final aspect of the shadowing included a short debriefing interview at the end of the completed shift, where we asked how typical the shift was, how they felt about it, and whether they felt like they got enough time with patients. This debrief provided incredible context to what was observed. Taken together, this four-part process allowed us to better understand the three features of a timescape (elaborated in chapter 2). These features guide my discussion below.

#1:   What is the *communication process* that Safety Net Healthcare wishes to support? What are the accompanying messages (i.e., *theories of communication*) about how best to achieve it?

Patient care, a multilayered and complex communication process, is central to the work of physicians everywhere. However, the theory of communication about the delivery of patient care (geared to prospective patients and other stakeholders) on the Safety Net Healthcare website differed to some extent from the actual processes that we observed in the clinic. It advertised the delivery of comprehensive and time-sensitive health care through patient–provider interactions. However, we observed a communication process where providers had inadequate time to meet patients' complex and multiple health-care needs and so had to settle for triaging the most important challenge(s) that patients faced and delay attention to other related problems. So, although the message shared with patients was to *expect comprehensive and time-sensitive health care*, the message to clinicians was that they should *keep the line moving*. Additionally, when physicians exceeded the time for clinic appointments in order to fully support patient care, through our ethnographic observations, we observed the personal and professional consequences of this decision, such as working through lunch, working after hours, and angry patients who had been kept waiting (as Montori predicts in *Why We Revolt*). Thus, we might elaborate this fast theory of communication to "Keep the line moving no matter what."

#2:   What is the *timescale* of this communication process?

As is the case with a lot of work in the service industry,[12] the stated communication process—in this case, comprehensive and time-sensitive health-care delivery—has a timescale that cannot be readily standardized. Despite this difficulty, at Safety Net Healthcare, every patient visit in primary care (i.e., internal medicine and family medicine) was allotted twenty minutes total, only a portion of which the physician gets to spend with their patient. A critical point to note about this guideline is that it is shaped by the Medicare[13] payment structure. External factors, such as industry norms,[14] drive a great deal of the inconsistency between written and practiced theories of chronemics. In chapter 4, I offer an extended case of how a child welfare movement has redesigned communication to align with the fundamental timescale of their work despite serious institutional constraints. At Safety Net Healthcare, however, this was not the case.

Upon learning of our general goal to better understand time in their work, several of the primary care physicians pointed to the standardized twenty minutes for all appointments as a huge source of frustration. They shared that different types of patients and different types of visits require different amounts of time to deliver high-quality health care. Far from expecting no time-based guidelines whatsoever, clinicians had very clear ideas about basic ways to redesign time in support of temporality. They instinctually identified a range of temporal processes that could be used to help determine the appropriate time frame for a visit.

For instance, they said that more time is needed with first-time patients than with established patients. There are two reasons for this.

First, communicating to build rapport (something critical when initially meeting a patient) can take more time than the same interaction with an established patient. This reflects understanding of the nonlinear relationship between time and communication consistent with slow communication design logics. Second, in the case of their underserved population, new patients often needed more time because they had often been waiting weeks or months to see someone after being released from hospital. Therefore, they were often more ill than established patients. Consequently, the clinician and patient needed more time to discuss the several health issues they faced. Several doctors also compared the time allotted to primary medicine with that allotted to specialty medicine and were incredulous that despite the longer list of medical needs to which they must attend in primary care, specialty medicine had longer (thirty-minute) appointments.

In short, because communication is a process, translating a service such as "delivery of patient care" into standardized units of time is less useful than determining an objective range that will successfully capture its subjective timescale. In the case of Safety Net, the communication process is comprehensive, time-sensitive health care. We observed that the lack of fit between the timescale of patient care (which ranges from less than to more than twenty minutes) and the time that doctors had to address patient care (twenty minutes total, much of it spent outside of the exam room ordering tests or coordinating care in other ways) meant that rather than offering "whole person" health, as Safety Net Healthcare advertises on its website, physicians were offering medical triage. Because triage arises in settings with inadequate (scarce) resources to care for all patients in a time-sensitive fashion, the lens of time scarcity illuminates the chronemic design of patient care at Safety Net Healthcare, elaborated through the last of three questions helpful in assessing chronemic design.

#3:   What *time-based assumptions and practices* support or obstruct this underlying communication process?

The considerable slippage between the timescale of patient care and the allotted time at Safety Net led to an experience of *scarcity* for all but one of the physicians we studied.[15] Most simply did not have enough time. Although they readily identified how more *flexible*[16] design strategies (based on either the type of patient or the type of visit) could support the temporality of their work, that was not the current design. Therefore, clinicians—that is, everyone on the health-care team led by the physicians we studied—had to modify their communication *with* patients and *about* patients to try and fit within the twenty minutes they were given.

To elaborate on this distinction, communication *with* patients includes time spent in exam rooms as well as communicating through the patient portal. Communication *about* patients occurs at the clinician's desk while coordinating with other health-care agencies (such as the hospital that released them) or their health-care teams (that might include a social worker, for example), just outside the exam room door, or after hours when completing paperwork. This work was hidden from the public-facing image of the doctor as being supported by a team of professionals that took care of everything outside of the exam room. This simply wasn't true. In addition to the work involved during the clinic time that we observed, one physician (by the pseudonym of Dr. Allen) shared that "what you'll observe during a specific clinic session may be the smallest portion of the time involved in prep and follow-up that is also part of a patient's care." So, the amount of work—before and after any one patient visit—was extensive by comparison to the twenty-minute appointment time slot.

During clinic, we were surprised to find that physicians themselves were required to spend a large portion of their time carrying out the administrative duties needed to coordinate patient care (e.g., talking with hospitals to get records, checking with pharmacies or medical equipment providers, etc.) and conferring with other members of the health-care team. Although the physicians were part of a team, their other team members were also visibly (and audibly) overwhelmed with the volume of work they had to do to support the doctors. As an example, team members faced persistent and routine technological problems when accessing electronic medical records. On one day during our observations, the entire electronic medical records system went offline. In an environment already defined by time scarcity due to patients' medical needs and the demand–capacity discrepancy to see patients in a timely fashion, slow and unreliable technology only heightened this experience.

One day early on in the study, I was time shadowing alone and stayed nearly until clinic close. When I conducted the debriefing interview with one physician (whom I will call Dr. Angela), she began to cry when describing the exhaustion and frustration associated with the structural conditions she faced in practicing medicine. We sat alone in her clinic cubicle that was—moments before—filled with a constant flow of interaction among the entire medical team (i.e., medical assistants, nurses, social workers, etc. during clinic hours), as this mid-career, energetic, well-liked doctor specializing in internal medicine talked about wanting to help patients while not having the organizational resources to do so. Despite her best countermeasures, coming to work still created a feeling of dread associated with facing the same insurmountable challenges day after day—that is, trying to improve the health of patients with multiple and complex health needs in the face of inadequate institutional resources. She contrasted the experience of scarcity at Safety Net with her work at another clinic where appointment times are thirty minutes, the patients and each member of their health-care team are all fully resourced, and, consequently, the patients receive better care (and are much healthier, despite it being an HIV clinic). She said it feels like a "vacation" on the days she works there compared to coming to Safety Net. She contrasted the "light" and "energetic" experience of working there with feeling like she's working with "weights on" during her shifts at Safety Net.

Dr. Angela also told us how the Safety Net approach to patient care costs more, despite the illusion of saving time and money. She gave the example of how depression—often presenting alongside other illnesses—is difficult to assess in the ten minutes[17] she gets with patients. She described a recent case where, while reviewing a patient chart, she noticed that her patient had been to the ER ten times complaining of chest pain. Each time, the patient was released from the ER after a battery of expensive tests that (fortunately) found no underlying heart problem. Dr. Angela decided to talk with her about the symptoms that kept sending her to the ER. Through a simple, thoughtful conversation that ended up lasting forty minutes, Dr. Angela discovered that the patient was having panic attacks and suffered from undiagnosed depression and anxiety. With this information, she was able to refer her to a mental health provider. The patient was successfully treated (including receiving appropriate medication) and did not visit the ER again. By taking extra time during one visit, she saved the larger Medicare health-care system (that employs her) an inordinate amount of money that would otherwise be spent on expensive, unnecessary tests and care. Thus, the prevailing fast theory of communication that guided Safety Net did not save time or money.

A Snapshot of Fast Communication Design Logics at Safety Net Healthcare

The communication-as-design at Safety Net was characterized by fast CDL in multiple regards:

- First, the design of appointments focused exclusively on a *single frame of interaction* in the present—that is, the most pressing health condition(s) assigned to a given appointment time slot—sometimes to the exclusion of a shared past or future. By past and future, I am not referring to the patient's health history and prognosis. In health care, this information is consulted in order to determine a medical course of action. Rather, I am referring to ways in which the clinician–patient interaction unfolds through a shared past and future. This includes whether they had already established a relationship, whether the patient is new to Safety Net in general, and more. Partnering to address long-term lifestyle issues not easily resolved in one visit may also be neglected in an appointment crowded with so much to do.

- In addition to the frame of interaction, the *perceived shape of the trajectory between time and interaction* was linear. The underlying presumption is that more time with a patient is too costly to make it worthwhile. The example of Dr. Angela diagnosing her patient's anxiety through taking more time suggests the poor fit of this perception in these sorts of health-care settings. The appointments were not designed to be responsive to larger challenges across systems (i.e., various aspects of the health-care system) or time (i.e., past, present, and future). Thus, a singular frame of interaction typically presumes a linear relationship between time and interaction.

- Similarly, the fundamental *belief about what interaction offers* is transactional. This belief informs the frame of interaction as well as the presumptive linear trajectory. It denies the transcendent possibilities available through interaction and instead sees appointments as simply a container to exchange information. It ignores the fundamental ambiguity of health care and the value of trust in doctor–patient relationships.

Reflecting on the Utility of Fast Communication Design Logics at Safety Net Healthcare

The study of Safety Net Healthcare offers an example of fast communication design utilized in a way that obstructs and degrades the underlying communication process it is intended to support. The high demand for services (i.e., a time-based phenomenon) drove the design of the work (i.e., a temporal phenomenon). This is never the basis of strong fast communication logics. Effective communication-as-design always begins with the communication process and then considers the role of time in supporting it. In contrast, the design at Safety Net ignored the temporal reality of patients, most of whom faced multiple and complex health diagnoses.

Although physicians routinely redesigned communication on the fly, it was a work-around to address the problems created by fast communication design logics. It led to some positive outcomes for the organization, but it also had negative personal and professional repercussions (e.g., angry patients who had been kept waiting, staff having to work through their lunch or after hours, etc.) because it ran against the prevailing design. It is not sustainable in the long term for high-quality work (in this case, patient care) or the organizational members responsible for it (in this case, physicians and the medical team). Notably, by the time we followed up with our participants when the study resumed post-COVID-19 lockdown, several had left Safety Net Health, including Dr. Angela—one of their most dedicated professionals. High rates of member turnover ultimately slow down work as new, on-boarded members face a steep learning curve in an already dysfunctional[18] system. Additionally, far before these members leave (as Dr. Angela confided during our interview), they are already burned out and exhausted, not operating at full capacity.

The challenges at Safety Net point to a fundamental challenge in various kinds of service work where organizations face inherent scarcity of resources. Triage, and even all-out avoidance (as we will discuss in the case of the Children's Advocacy Centers of Texas [CACTX] in chapter 4), is a natural reaction to the problem. However, triage is only a short-term solution for unexpected situations. The challenge that Safety Net faced was neither short term nor unexpected.

Safety Net Reprise: Refocusing the Lens to Redesign for Slow Communication Design Logics

Rather than designing work through the lens of scarcity, it is essential to shift the lens toward potential solutions to scarcity. The other lenses through which physicians at Safety Net redesigned their own work in an ad hoc fashion suggest an alternative redesign. For instance, Dr. Angela used a *future-focused* lens to consider how to help the patient who had been to the ER with unexplained chest pains. It saved the patient and broader organization a great deal of time in the future. However, it did not address her own scheduling problems. In fact, on its own, a future focus came at the cost of delaying her entire schedule. Aside from the short-term stress that delays can cause, organizational members who face chronic delays in their work are also less satisfied with the quality of communication and relationships at work.[19]

Therefore, in terms of systemic change, she and several colleagues wanted the organization to consider different needs and different patients through different appointment times. This points to the benefits of using a more *flexible* lens to design patient care. In order to more fully understand why emphasizing flexibility may be invaluable in this clinic redesign, I offer an example and concept from behavioral economics and psychology on scarcity. It has to do with what Mullainathan and Shafir (whom I mentioned in chapter 2) call the "bandwidth tax"—a reduction in our thinking capacity that ultimately slows work.[20] This tax is why, as explained in chapter 1, one cannot simply go faster (i.e., pick up the *pace*) to get more done. They explain, "When we experience scarcity of any kind, we become absorbed by it. The mind orients automatically, powerfully, toward unfulfilled needs. . . . Scarcity is more than just the displeasure of having very little. It changes how we think."[21] This is why fast CDL cannot be the default strategy for speed: Our biology is not built to sustain it. Thus, part of the chronemic problem of scarcity is its tie to a cognitive phenomenon.

As an example of the poor fit that fast CDL offers as a long-term solution, Mullainathan and Shafir describe a cardiothoracic surgery department that, like Safety Net, addressed the need for their services by simply having surgical teams increase the number of patients treated. Initially, this allowed the department to treat more patients faster. However, it also led to an increase in patient deaths (beyond what could be attributed to the larger number of patients), suggesting cognitive impairment. What is more, in addition to the higher death rate, eventually the department also saw a decrease in speed. It took even longer than it originally had to manage each patient. From a fast CDL, taking up all of the slack and having people work more hours is beneficial initially, but across industries, the benefits are soon lost to this cognitive tax.

From a chronemic design perspective, responding to scarcity by creating slack to reduce this bandwidth tax means decreasing the pace through increasing flexibility. Rather than attempt to utilize all available moments through taking up all of the slack (i.e., extra time) left in any appointment, create more "give," or flexibility, in the system and allow even more time to do the work. This is precisely what physicians at Safety Net were asking for in order to do their jobs better. Creating more flexibility and reducing the pace around patient care would allow clinicians to address nonroutine events when needed. Instead, they often triaged or avoided patient needs altogether by engaging in leave-taking behaviors (e.g., looking down at their watch, walking away, opening the door) to keep appointments on schedule, a classic fast communication design logic at work. This natural avoidance mirrors the neglect (and increased patient death) that occurred in the cardiothoracic surgery department when there was no slack.

Mullainathan and Shafir give an example of how an acute care hospital resolved the problem of too few available operating rooms by creating more slack in their surgery planning. Through recognizing that the problem of capacity originated with nonroutine events (i.e., emergency surgeries), an adviser suggested that the hospital leave one surgical room unscheduled to accommodate these unplanned surgeries. This slack provided them with the flexible design needed to accommodate emergencies, enabling them to accommodate more surgical cases and generate more revenue. In effect, they addressed the problem of scarcity through introducing more flexibility in their existing scheduling practices. They did not have to increase their speed (more surgeries per unit of time), which would require more bandwidth. Rather, they both decreased the speed *and* did more surgeries simultaneously. Following from a slow CDL, they "went slow to go fast" through introducing scheduling flexibility into the chronemic design, illustrating how shifting time-based lenses is key to redesign. As described in chapter 2, design frames through the timescale and time dimensions that guide it. Therefore, enlarging the timescale (to capture nonroutine events such as an emergency surgery) and refocusing on flexibility over scarcity shifted the underlying CDLs.

The American Football Timescape: Moving from Inconsistent to Competing Theories

In addition to inconsistent theories of communication (especially between external and internal communication), organizational members frequently navigate *competing theories of communication* as well. This competition often occurs within internal communication. As described below, I observed competing theories while studying American football. These competing theories reflected career dynamics that professionals face across a range of organizations, including at Safety Net Healthcare. For instance, as part of our early research at Safety Net, I spoke with a psychiatrist (Dr. Chris) who helps medical students manage their career demands and prevent burnout. She shared that it felt futile to recommend lifestyle changes to clients that their work simply would not allow. Although she let them know that

The American football timescape
Professional socialization

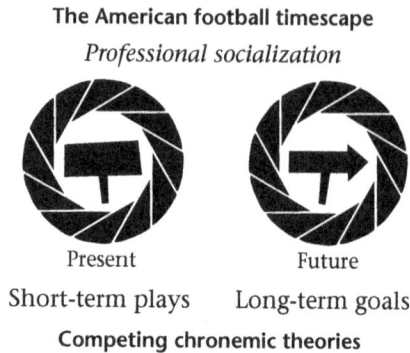

Present   Future
Short-term plays   Long-term goals
Competing chronemic theories

Figure 3.2
The American football timescape.

things such as working fewer hours and unplugging at home were helpful to manage burnout, she knew that—based on the other messages they received about how to be successful in medical school—it was simply not possible if they wanted to succeed in their chosen path. These two messages—one conveyed by the psychiatrist ("Create healthy boundaries around work") and the other by organizational leaders ("Success comes through long hours and sacrifice")—are in direct competition with each other. In order to follow one path, it is necessary to abandon the other. They are mutually exclusive.

Versions of these same two messages and their competing communication design logics are prevalent, even celebrated, in many professions. An underlying narrative that valorizes sacrifice (like the missed lunches we saw and heard about as well as the nonstop pace we observed at Safety Net) often competes with a narrative of work–life balance. As described previously, as *employees*, the physicians at Safety Net lived the experience of inconsistent CDLs. The organization failed to do what it sought (and Montori would argue "ought") to do. However, beyond the inconsistency between the messages that clients and employees received, there was another conflict. As *professionals*, the physicians also lived the experience of competing theories. To give what was needed to the organization required lowering their quality of life. As some evidence of this, physicians were part of the pandemic-era Great Resignation. Because of the toll their careers often take on their life many were, "stepping back and saying, 'Is this the life I want to be leading?'"[22]

Similarly, when we returned to Safety Net two years later to conduct exit interviews, more than half of the physicians we had studied (and many others whom we had not directly shadowed) had resigned because of the stressors of the job. Dr. Allen (mentioned in the last section) politely declined our request for a final interview and summed it up in this way: "I'm finished with all this and will retire in a couple of months. Dr. A is moving on as well. And Drs. B, C, X, and Y before us. . . . I think an interview would just leave me explaining ad nauseum the bitterness and disappointments I feel. And I really don't want to stew in that anger any longer. I hope you understand, and I hope you can carry on with your project anyway."

This was an optional retirement by a deeply dedicated professional who made the difficult decision to address his personal well-being by leaving Safety Net. Therefore, in the American football case, I shift focus from exploring whether there is a match between internal versus external communication design logics to considering how multiple, competing communication design logics impact an organization and its members. Although I generally study how communication design impacts our ability to get work done, the personal costs have also loomed large in my findings. Questions about these costs and how to minimize them drove my interest in studying American football. In this research project, I explored how the communication design of work impacted the professionals performing it.

Particularly, given the importance of timescale in evaluating the efficacy of chronemic design, I wanted to understand the outcomes for professionals *across the lifespan*, not just in their years of gainful employment. This is because our work, although a means to earn income, also has implications for our "selves." For instance, working the graveyard shift for too many years has been found to shorten individuals' lifespans.[23] We also know that content moderators (e.g., those individuals who must personally view online content to screen out images of child pornography and extremely violent depictions) suffer from incredible vicarious trauma.[24] And, of course, from the beginning of human civilization, soldiers have brought home the physical and emotional wounds of their work.[25] So, we take our work with us beyond the time with which we are engaged in it. This reflects the larger temporal experience of our work outside of a given task.

Data Collection: Learning About Communication-as-Design in American Football

To understand the timescape of American football from multiple perspectives (i.e., individual and institutional), from 2011 to 2013, my research team and I held informant[26] interviews with eighty-five professionals, including current National Football League (NFL) players, retired NFL players, National Collegiate Athletic Association (NCAA) players, NFL coaches, NCAA coaches, athletic directors, and front office staff. I also drew from conversation and correspondence with sociologist and civil rights activist Dr. Harry Edwards, professor emeritus at the University of California, Berkeley, and longtime consultant on player development for multiple NFL teams. Together, this range of perspectives allowed me to see the broader organizational communication processes that drive this profession as well as its ethical and practical implications.

In many respects, this work is an exception. As an example, in the earliest phases of this research project, I visited the National Institute for Occupational Safety and Health, the federal agency responsible for conducting research and making recommendations for the prevention of work-related injury, illness, disability, and death. When I asked about research funding opportunities given the prevalence of chronic traumatic encephalopathy (CTE) among football players, the program officer nearly laughed. A kind man who was simply caught off guard, his reaction reminded me what people immediately think of when professional football comes to mind. First, because the work is glamorized, the risks are minimized and downplayed as the cost of the profession. Second, part of that glamour comes from the remarkable images of power (physical, financial, and otherwise) associated with the work. As one NFL player I interviewed (by the pseudonym of New Earth) described it is "the last gladiator sport because, I mean, it's going to be fifty to sixty thousand people coming to see, you know, other guys ripping another guy's head off." Indeed, it is an exception in many ways, and the long-term costs of being a gladiator, to borrow New Earth's metaphor, initially drew my attention.

However, over the two years I spent studying these professionals, I realized that its profound temporal exceptions allow it to magnify subtle, overlooked chronemic design features shared across many professions. Because of the stark physicality of the work, we can easily see (and informants told us) that the impact of the work stays with players for a lifetime. Notably, at the time of our interviews, more new and damning scientific evidence had surfaced showing that chronic traumatic encephalopathy (CTE), a progressive neurological brain disorder, was found in the brains of many collegiate and professional players.[27] Once I understood how the designable features of time can mask this danger, I saw similarities across industries about how "stuff" gets broken, as per Zuckerberg's mantra. It may not be broken as quickly (i.e., three years—the average NFL career) in other professions or as permanently (i.e., CTE), but the communication design logics that guide career development in other professions also valorize breaking stuff.

To support a balanced perspective as we engaged in the study, I selected members of the research team[28] so as to include outsiders (such as myself—interested in the work of the football but not at all in the game), insiders (including collegiate players with close family members who played in the NFL and who understand fundamental aspects of the game), and fans (these members of the research team were enthusiasts with knowledge of the game but no personal experiences). This range of contributions to the project were valuable during our discussions of the data and also helped us in reaching out and securing informant interviews with a wide range of football professionals. We began by identifying individuals through our personal networks as well as introductions through the Texas Program in Sports and Media (now the Center for Sports Communication and Media) at the University of Texas. At the conclusion of each interview, we asked each informant to suggest a colleague or friend in the field of professional or collegiate football who might also be open to an interview. This was an effective way to broaden our sample geographically, covering collegiate players and NFL professionals with careers spanning the West, North, South, and East regions of the United States.

#1: What is the *communication process* that supports individual football players in their careers? What are the accompanying messages (i.e., *theories of communication*) about how best to achieve it?

Through the varied temporal lenses of retired, current, and aspiring players as well as their coaches and support staff, I found that the primary communication process upon which players rely to guide their careers on and off the field is a complex, long-term process called "professional socialization." Professional socialization teaches us how to be a good professional through on-the-job experiences. It spans any one organization and is part of a larger institution guided by its own communication design logics that provide answers to questions such as: How should I behave? How should I think? How should I perform to my fullest potential? This ongoing process begins prior to becoming a member (e.g., while working toward the goal of becoming a professional player), and it is tightly bound up with an interrelated process called "identification," where members gradually shift from a sense of "me" to "we." Sociologist Robert W. Turner II describes what this identity looks like for NFL players: "Only a certain kind of athlete can make it in the NFL. Gaining entry . . . is not solely a reflection of a player's level of commitment, physical talents, work ethic, or devotion to the sport. The winning ticket holder in the NFL lottery is a player who displays a combination of all of these characteristics as well as a complete adoption of . . . a way of thinking about and acting . . . to the degree that they believe no sacrifice is too great."[29]

Through our interviews, we found that two competing CDLs (fast and slow) dominated the professional socialization of football players telling them how to be good players. The fast design logic—held especially by NCAA Division I personnel and in the NFL—was to "leave it all out on the field." The slow design logic—held especially by NCAA Division II staff and high school coaches—was to "plan for a future on and off of the field." Sometimes, these competing messages came from different sources. Sometimes, they were shared by the same source, each alongside the other. Players readily shared the role of coaches, other organizational leadership, and senior players in shaping both their work on the field as well as their understanding of their larger role as a professional.

#2:   What is the *timescale* of this communication process?

The timescale at which one *demonstrates mastery of being a professional* was cast in two very different ways in our interviews. In one, the communication process was limited to an on-field performance (i.e., a brief timescale). In the other, it supported players over an entire career or longer (i.e., a long timescale). These two ways of being compete for adherents. We heard stories of how this professional socialization process begins on the first day of practice. Collegiate coaching staff would imitate the formal NCAA and university admonition that "school comes first and athletics come second" by mocking this language and, instead, form a number two with their hands when mouthing the words "first" and a number one while mouthing the word "second." Thus, early on for many collegiate players, demonstrating and delivering on one's professional identity was set on a timescale determined by the game—as brief as the current play and as extended as their eligibility to play for the team. This message even came with a preemptive warning that others will tell them to build it with different priorities.

Other coaches and staff framed the timescale of a player's professional identity development and delivery as extended across a lifetime. For example, when asked about his main goal for players, an NCAA Division II coach (by the pseudonym of Tiger) explained:

> The first objective is, is for them to graduate college . . . I've coached thirty-one and I've had twenty-nine graduated . . . the football aspect of it handles itself because that's what they come to do. . . . The satisfaction going to into the (winning)? That comes and goes, but the lifelong relationships that I have, and I will continue to have that. . . . The satisfaction is to see them walk across the stage and become the first one in their families to graduate. The satisfaction is to get a wedding invitation from them seven years after I've coached them . . . To get a letter from them when—say now they are successful coach, or successful businessman, and they say that—you know I or we were principally responsible for their success, that's why.

Within this communication design logic, being a former player with successes off the field—having a good life—was part of what football offers.

#3:   What *time-based assumptions and practices* support or obstruct these underlying communication processes?

Assumptions about the present and future were central to players' conceptions and performances of their professional identity. In order to engage in the sheer physicality of the work, players must be present-time focused. A former NCAA player who was working in the front office for an NFL team at the time of his interview (by the pseudonym of AB) explained:

> People just look at football and think, you know I'm going to make it. And part of the challenge is that you *have* to have that mentality

to succeed. You *have* to believe that you are the best, um, to make it, and you *really* have to believe it. When I walked on the field, I was convinced that I was the *best* thing ever. And I'm not going to, and, and, and I don't think its bragging, I just honestly believed that I was the best player on that field, and nobody could stop me. Nobody could stop me. So, it, it, it's hard to balance that (future-focus) with you know, "I'm the best." and you know, "Do I really need school? I'm the best. I'm going to make it." You know?

In contrast, BJ, the pseudonym for a retired player who played in the NFL for five years before becoming a broadcast sports analyst, explained the future-focused, slow communication version of success: "Pay attention to plan B. 'Cause we all thought we were invincible, we all thought we'd play forever, and it just doesn't work out that way for the majority." Similarly, an athletic director (by the pseudonym of Buddy Rich) described the future-focus that it was his job to share: "Anything that lets them know that it's okay to be something other than the football player is a good thing because eventually you're going to be something other than a football player . . . often times when I talk to guys they think they have to be one or the other . . . They don't know that they can be a great football player . . . but also be these other things." So, rather than the present focus being problematic, it becomes an issue only when it is not complemented by a future-focus CDL.

A Snapshot of Fast Communication Design Logics in American Football

The communication-as-design in American football is characterized by fast CDL in multiple regards. Although speed is essential to the game, the CDLs that drive professional socialization do not have to be. Nonetheless, much of the communication reflects a fast design logic.

- *What is the time frame of the interaction?* To demonstrate their commitment to a set of professional ideals, players are told to "leave it all out on the field." In a general and light-hearted context, this expression simply means to work very hard in the pursuit of one's goals. However, in a more specific and professionalized context where early socialization messages are to place athletics above everything else, then this message takes on a more literal meaning. Ultimately, the focus on a *single frame of interaction* (i.e., in the present) drives the design of many aspiring and professional careers. Barbarian, the pseudonym of an informant who played eleven seasons in the NFL, referenced the storied example of Ronnie Lott getting his finger amputated in order to continue in a game. Others echoed a focus on this single frame of interaction more broadly and pointed to the general neglect of all aspects of life other than one's career—including attention to one's long-term relationships, health, and finances. Notably, this neglect is an aspect of the classic Type A behavior pattern shared by many.[30]

- *What is the perceived shape of the trajectory between time and interaction?* Although coaches are willing to spend massive amounts of time in reviewing film (those we interviewed worked incredibly long hours, weeks, and seasons), the focus of my research was not on the CDL of winning football games. Given my interest in an ethical, sustainable professional environment for the players, I was interested in the perceived shape of the trajectory between time and interaction as it concerns professional development. Although the NFL publicly declares "The NFL's commitment to players' long-term health and well-being extends on and off of the field, for every player, through all stages of their career . . . advancing the resources available to players to equip them with the tools they need to succeed over the course of their lives," multiple players told us that this had not been their experience. One then-current NFL player, by the pseudonym of Tee, who spoke to us during the 2011 Lockout (a more than four-month work stop-page caused by conflict over a new collective bargaining agree-ment), explained that their goals are opposed to the player's goal by definition: "Coaches in high school probably like generally care about you . . . The League . . . it's just about keeping their job." As a result, communication as an investment in players is treated as a *linear relationship*. A nonlinear relationship would require some basic level of goal alignment (such as Tiger's account of his long-term relationship with players) beyond on-field performance.

- *What is the underlying belief about what human interaction offers?* It was abundantly clear that players and coaches both believed in the possibilities of transcendence through human interaction. Coaches such as Tiger certainly exemplify this transcendence. In the NFL, however, this was largely focused on performance as it relates to winning games. One informant by the pseudonym of TT, who played in the NFL for ten seasons and earned a Super Bowl title, described: "I was fortunate with that and the NFL I was blessed to have some of the greatest coaches you know that ever coached the game. Tom Landry: I spent two years with him. Knew the game offense and defense. Was one of the best minds that the game ever had. Jimmy Johnson, no question, one of the best moti-vators that I've ever had." However, beyond winning games, as Tee describes above, the relationship is transactional—it's "a business relationship." This is a key point of the American football case. The possibility of transcendence through professional develop-ment is precluded because the organization's and the individual's needs are at odds with one another.

Reflecting on the Utility of Fast Communication Design Logics in American Football

The case of contemporary American football illuminates a funda-mental challenge with fast CDLs used in contexts where long-term vital outcomes are at stake. Zuckerberg's idea of "breaking stuff" may sound innocuous without specific reference to what gets broken, but when we cast a spotlight on what breaks, its ethical and political implications are clarified. As mentioned previously, debates about the future of work and well-being in the NFL were put on the national stage during the 2011 lockout. My research team was collecting data in the field right before, during, and immediately after the lockout, and we asked players about it. The eleven-year NFL veteran, who gave himself the pseudonym Barbarian, offers a pointed explanation that we heard from the retired players:

> Jim McMahon says he can't remember why he goes in the
> room. Terry Bradshaw says he can't remember anything he did
> yesterday . . . this is why the NFL does everything they possibly can
> to try to stay ahead of this because one guy somewhere is going to
> win a lawsuit about what football does to us. Because right now, the
> way the system is set up, they just deny us and deny us and deny us
> and hope we die. So, we're coal miners. . . . I've had six teammates
> die in the last three years. . . . that's the ugly legacy of football.
> All the wonder and joy of machismo and fight and all that good
> stuff, but unless you're really lucky, really lucky you're going to be
> screwed up for the rest of your life.

Barbarian's reference to coal mining ties the issues he and others experience in professional football to larger issues and concerns about where the well-being of the employee is positioned in fast CDLs more broadly. Through a focus on single frames of interaction, linear trajectories, and transactional relationships, the tie to well-being is absent at the most basic level.

Of course, there are many obvious differences between coal miners and professional football players. Status and salary are chief among them. Informants explained how incredibly variable these commodities are, however. Aside from the fluidity of status, informants shared the inside joke that NFL stands for "Not For Long" because professional football careers are so short (typically three years). When divided by the average number of years most Americans will work (i.e., forty-two years),[31] this amounts to about $61K annually in 2023.[32] Given the extraordinary cost of medical care to manage lifelong professional injuries they shared with us, these were not wealthy individuals. Instead, former players told us that access to health care drove their interest in collective bargaining negotiations. Additionally, one of our informants was part of the practice squad that accounts for 20 percent of NFL players who train, travel, and practice with the team but rarely play. When they do play, they earn very little ($11,500 a week in 2023), and that might be it for the year. The promise of more, however, is what keeps them on the squad.

Thus, although there are short-term differences, these should not obscure Barbarian's point that the work itself is what exposes both miners and players to the very dangers that the organization continually downplays, denies, and then delays taking responsibility for in real terms. His predictions would also come true, at least partly. The NFL ultimately settled a billion-dollar concussion lawsuit[33] brought against them by former players and led by one of the men (Jim McMahon) he talked about in his interview. Nonetheless, a decade after the initial settlement (at the time this book went to press), only 6.5 percent of the claims had been paid, despite 60 percent of them having a qualifying diagnosis. Indeed, national broadcast coverage[34] of the visible danger and consequences associated with professional football allows us to see what happens behind the scenes of fast CDLs. Although games are won or lost in seconds, the bodies that make those wins or suffer those losses continue to experience the effects of those plays for a lifetime.

Reflecting on the chronemic design that shapes the institution of football exposes a fundamental similarity across professions. Institutions across industries tend to prefer, invest in, and reward those members who proverbially "leave it all out on the field"—a short-term, present-focused assumption.[35] Fast CDLs normalize this sacrifice. This was exemplified by a distinction players shared with us about the difference between being "hurt" versus "injured." Being hurt is the default, and it doesn't stop work. Being injured means that you have been carried off the field by medics, and it's the only thing that stops work. A version of this distinction underlies the communication design logic of work across industries. Sometimes, this message is tied to the status associated with a job (e.g., NFL, Silicon Valley, physicians), and other times it is not (e.g., shift work, coal mining, content moderation). Nonetheless, it competes with the practical needs of organizational members to take a long-term, future-focused approach and preserve their own "self" that exists apart from the organization. This includes attention to their own emotional and physical well-being as well as their personal and familial relationships. In comparison with the fast communication design logic on public display in American football, for others—that is, the physicians who left Safety Net under the weight of the chronemic design—the reality is privately suffered.

The Everyday Digital Communication Timescape: Managing Chronemic Urgency

Thus far, I have described how fast communication design logics often drive the day-to-day work of organizations and institutions alongside *inconsistent* and *competing* "feel good" slow chronemic theories shared with external stakeholders. That is, organizations often create public messaging around slow communication design logics because, frankly, it sounds good. However, in practice, the day-to-day frontline organizing in these same institutions draws on fast CDLs that fail members and their organizations because they are inappropriate for much of the work they do. I have offered examples of both practical and ethical reasons that fast CDL is a poor fit for many of the communication demands organizations must navigate.

Despite the common failures associated with fast CDLs illustrated in the two previous case studies, they are indispensable for accomplishing time-sensitive communication. At a fundamental level, to be effective, communication must be timely.[36] With more and more

The everyday digital communication timescape

Responsiveness

Urgency	Delay
Aiming for immediate or prompt responses	Not delaying a response to avoid forgetting

Complementary chronemic theories

Figure 3.3
The everyday digital communication timescape.

communication demands across our personal and professional lives, however, this can be a challenge. Therefore, in the present case, I show how multiple chronemic theories—one fast and one slow—actually work well alongside each other when they have internal consistency and complementarity. Rather than being at odds, or this case study being the exception, both fast and slow CDLs are needed as part of a holistic design to accomplish time-sensitive communication.

Fast communication design logics are valuable because there are settings and contexts where communication processes *must* fit into the available time if they are to be successful. For example, in the case of a call with an emergency services operator/dispatcher (such as 911 in the United States), time *should* drive the communication. It must initially be focused on a single frame of interaction (i.e., the present). These are moments when communication has a linear relationship with time—that is, it comes at an absolute cost. Therefore, organizations and individuals reduce communication to the most essential information in order to keep the task moving. In these cases, transactional interactions are prioritized. Individuals need to exchange information as quickly as possible. Relationships may not be essential to the work. In exceptional cases, relationships may develop, depending upon the specific scenario and how long it lasts, but for most calls, this is an impediment to the primary task.

In the twenty-first century, these same issues arise daily in communication settings where life and death do not hang in the balance. Keeping up with email for work, personal text messages on multiple platforms, and social media messages via a number of applications—all while making sure that we can be reached quickly when it matters—demands that we oscillate between fast and slow communication design logics across digital and colocated settings. This is a fundamental challenge in our everyday lives because fast communication proliferates easily, given the low cost and effort to produce it as well as how quickly it is consumed.[37] Therefore, our communication-as-design must offer an efficient way to navigate multiple streams of digital conversation and respond quickly to urgent communication needs.

Data Collection: Learning About Communication-as-Design in Everyday Digital Communication

Fellow chronemics scholar, Yoram Kalman, spent two of his research sabbaticals at the University of Texas at Austin in order to pursue potential collaborations. We share an interest in practical and theoretical questions about how the day-to-day rhythm of communication from multiple streams (phone, text, social media, email, etc.) is established and maintained. So, we wanted to know if people followed particular rules or norms in everyday life that make it more likely to be reached urgently (by certain people or in certain situations) when it matters. If so, were they explicit about these rules, and if not, how did we learn them? We wondered exactly how and why certain messages were privileged and how widely this logic was shared across people.

We ultimately coined the term "chronemic urgency" to measure (and compare) the urgency that users assign to certain messages they send and receive via a variety of communication media they use. Thus, the everyday digital communication case explores chronemic urgency and the implicit rules that people observe to be timely when it matters most. Our first study consisted of eighteen semi-structured interviews—led by our collaborator Ana Aguilar—that lasted between forty-two and sixty minutes. It focused exclusively on Generation Z, given the greater range of media they were likely to use. The findings from this phase were then used to inform a second study that used a survey method and included 773 generationally diverse respondents (Generation Z, Millennials, Generation X, and Baby Boomers) across three groups.

#1:   What is *the communication process* that everyday digital communication needs to support? What are the accompanying messages (i.e., *theories of communication*) about how best to achieve it?

Time-sensitive responsiveness is an essential aspect of the communication process in general, and its role in digital communication has been studied extensively. For instance, Kalman and colleagues[38] analyzed more than a hundred and fifty thousand responses in various types of online communication[39] to understand the speed at which people responded. Through calculating the average delay in responding via digital media, they found three response zones (I, II, and III) that reflected the same underlying rhythm of responses seen (and expected) in face-to-face communication: zone I is fast, zone II is a pause, and zone III is silent.

Kalman and fellow communication scholar Sheizaf Rafaeli later conducted an experiment about the impact of non-responsiveness (i.e., pauses and silence) in digital communication for job candidates.[40] Consistent with their hypothesis, participants expected strong candidates to reply quickly (zone I). When a candidate who was initially favored failed to respond immediately, it hurt perceptions of their relationship, evaluations of their fitness for the job, and their credibility. This suggests that we expect competent communicators to be timely communicators. Put differently, being responsive to urgent messages is important to accomplish basic individual and collective goals.

#2:   What is the *timescale* of this communication process?

The timescale of these zones varies across context. In real-time (synchronous) communication, such as what occurs face-to-face, this ranges from less than a second (fast or zone I) to 9.7 seconds or less (slow or zone II) to 10 seconds or more (silence or zone III). Because digital communication has the affordance of being asynchronous (i.e., people do not have to communicate at the same time)—the norms of responsiveness in email stretch out from a day (i.e., fast) to ten days (i.e., slow), and must reach more than ten days before considered silent.

#3: What *time-based assumptions and practices* support this underlying communication process?

This case study centers on culturally-based assumptions about urgency and practices around delay and how these lenses shape our communication and relationships. Across time and contexts, *when* we communicate has been an important part of *what* we communicate.[41] Thus, our research team asked interview and survey participants (M-Turk workers, undergraduates, and administrators) how others could get in touch with them urgently. Participants shared that messages received through certain media are (1) used for urgent communication, (2) checked more often, (3) more likely to be used by others who wish to contact the user urgently, and (4) more likely to lead to a quicker response. Our findings point to a general responsiveness imperative, or a norm of responding as soon as possible to every message that requires an answer and minimizing delay. This imperative is driven by two concerns that privilege urgency: (1) wanting to avoid an inappropriate delay that creates the impression of ignoring the sender, and (2) wanting to avoid forgetting to respond later.

A Snapshot of Fast Communication Design Logics in Everyday Digital Communication

In both of our studies, we found that across varied populations and generations (from Gen Z to Baby Boomers), people assign the highest chronemic urgency to phone calls (mobile and landline) and text messages. Ratings for the fourteen media identified by our participants and included in the survey are illustrated in table 3.2. This observation reflects the first starting point of communication-as-design: Design is a natural fact about communication. In everyday life, people are creative problem solvers who draw on mutual knowledge and shared rules of interaction. These were not typically explicit conventions, although sometimes they were.

For example, in addition to fast CDLs driving the messages associated with high chronemic urgency, the same beliefs about how time-sensitive communication should operate also occasionally informed their strategies for responding to messages that respondents rated as having low chronemic urgency. Macarena5, a Gen Z interview participant, explains how she assigns low chronemic urgency to messages when she wants to moderate how interested she appears. In this example, she disguises the fact that she's read a Snapchat message to appear less available and, hence, in greater demand:

Macarena5: You have to turn on airplane mode, open the Snapchat, delete the application, turn back on the Internet, install the application, and log in again. It's a whole process that really makes you think like, "Is it really worth it going through the whole process just to avoid that person knowing that you saw a Snapchat at the time that you did?"

Interviewer: This is just so that they don't know when you opened it?

Macarena5: It's just so that they don't know that you opened it. Or if you want to see it right away, but you need to give it a couple of hours not to show that much interest. So you would go through that process.

Because not responding in a timely fashion to another is seen as (near) universally rude, Macarena5 uses this strategy to avoid being seen as rude (while also not readily available). While this may be a common norm in new romantic relationships, it varies by context. In an interview setting, another Gen Z participant with the pseudonym of Barbara7 described the opposite strategy. She explained, "I would get back to people within two minutes or three minutes. . . . like, I actually look at my email as opposed to some people who I guess take forever to respond. . . . I just wanted to get information across quickly, so I looked like I was put together or something." In both instances, the message design logic reflects the idea of time as a commodity that can be saved or spent.

As some evidence that respondents used fast communication design logics to complement slow communication design logics, we found that the relationship between sender and receiver generally determined whether exclusively fast CDLs were used or whether they were used in the service of slow CDLs in the long term. In new or long-term relationships, fast CDLs were often used in the service of slow CDLs. Individuals reported using fast CDLs as a part of relational maintenance or development (e.g., in order to make or a maintain a favorable impression). The interview story that Barbara7 recounted reflects this interdependent relationship. In contrast, in superficial business or professional relationships, such as coordinating an appointment, a fast CDL was the exclusive design logic used (i.e., in order to avoid forgetting). This explains the wide range of urgencies assigned by different users to each medium, especially pronounced in messages sent via medium and low chronemic urgency media (e.g., email, WhatsApp, Snapchat) where the consensus was low (reflected in the high standard deviations). Additionally, even for mobile phoning and texting, there is no full consensus (evidenced by the standard deviation of 0.3–0.4).

Ultimately, the timescape of everyday digital communication was characterized by fast CDL in multiple regards:

- *What is the time frame of the interaction?* As a process, responsiveness relies upon sustained attention to a single frame of

Table 3.2
Chronemic agency of fourteen communication media across three groups

Medium	Mean Chronemic Agency (MTurks)	Mean Chronemic Agency (Undergrads)	Mean Chronemic Agency (Administrators)
Mobile	85.57	89.01	90.55
Text	72.06	76.52	84.50
Landline	70.53	—	58.06
WhatsApp	58.69	53.97	—
Facetime	57.18	55.24	35.32
Skype	45.2	—	—
FB messenger	45.19	37.03	23.57
Slack	42.09	42.25	—
email	35.58	58.98	62.63
Snapchat	21.11	33.00	10.81
Twitter	19.54	26.63	22.54
FB wall	17.72	22.22	10.49
Instagram	15.66	18.49	11.38
LinkedIn	14.90	23.64	9.79

Notes: Media sorted from highest to lowest chronemic agency (CA) of MTurk group. Missing cells in undergrads' and administrators' columns due to small sample ($n < 20$). FB: Facebook.

interaction: the present. Even in long-term relationships that have a past and future, responsiveness is defined by what happens in this single frame of interaction.

- *What is the perceived shape of the trajectory between time and interaction?* Responsiveness operates through a linear relationship between time and interaction. That is, communication costs time. Thus, in order to effectively manage the most urgent messages from the most important senders, people privilege certain media over others. Brevity is also used in these settings to make the communication fit the time available.

- *What is the underlying belief about what human interaction offers?* The assignment of chronemic urgency and its related responsiveness imperative is tied to human interaction as transactional. It does not mean that fast communication design logics can never be transcendent, but this occurs principally when they are used alongside slow communication design logics. Transcendence is better supported by nonlinear trajectories and multiple time frames.

Reflecting on the Utility of Fast Communication Design Logics in Everyday Digital Communication

Fast communication design logics are time focused and, as such, are an incredibly efficient communication design. This makes them an indispensable coordinative tool, including navigating logistic interactions. Additionally, they are best leveraged in the service of interactions that reflect slow communication design logics. This is exemplified by McKenzieEmery13:

Interviewer: When you're deciding that you are going to respond to these calls, how quickly do you tend to respond?

McKenzieEmery13: Immediately or I forget.

Interviewer: Can you tell me of a time when you should have answered or returned a phone call more quickly but did not?

McKenzieEmery13: Yeah. A couple of weeks ago, my grandfather called me twice, and I forgot to call him back. Then, he surprised me, he was coming to [the city where the campus is based]. He was in [the city], I didn't know. I still saw him, but I had plans that I had to cancel because I had to go see my grandfather.

Interviewer: Why did you not answer or return the call quickly?

McKenzieEmery13: I was busy and then forgot to call him back.

Thus, fast CDLs thrive at managing the responsiveness needed for both one-time and long-term interactions.

Note that precisely because fast CDLs are so useful for facilitating coordination, it is critical to be intentional about when they are employed. Their efficiency can take on an inertial quality so that they become the default design for interactions. The same urgency that we assign to messages in order to manage information overload and the impressions we make also exerts a wider influence. It hurts our ability to focus and get "deep work"[42] done because we allow the messages to interrupt our work. It allows us to coordinate efficiently in many settings, strategically in some settings, and mindlessly in other settings.

As more and more of our interaction becomes digital, we lose a great deal of everyday "friction," or time-based inefficiency, and risk losing sight of its value. In fact, *The New York Times* documented a trend of using meal-replacement drinks in Silicon Valley to improve efficiency: "The time wasted by eating is, in Silicon Valley parlance, a 'pain point' even for the highest echelon of techie.[43] We risk losing sight of the value of what sociologist Eviatar Zerubavel calls "temporal landmarks,"[44] such as a popular television show that people traditionally stopped everything to watch (that is now streaming 24-7 on Netflix) or an office lunch break (that people may skip to eat at their desks, given remote work arrangements). These everyday frictions such as meals with colleagues and shared television viewing support the nonlinear trajectories, multiple time frames, and transcendence upon which slow CDLs rely.

Summary

Time, as a design for communication, took center stage as the ultimate path to task accomplishment during the early twentieth century, replacing many temporally based rhythms in work. Facilitated by the invention and diffusion of electric light (which made daylight superfluous as an arbiter of work) as well as the widespread availability of inexpensive, reliable wristwatches, work became disconnected from temporality in a substantial way (especially as compared to agrarian work). When labor became inextricably tied to time, it fundamentally changed what work meant. In the 1936 silent film about industrialism, *Modern Times*, Charlie Chaplin dramatized this shift. The main character, the Little Tramp, had every aspect of his temporal existence increasingly subject (and subjugated) to time. Not only was the Little Tramp outpaced by an accelerated mechanical assembly line, he almost choked while being force-fed lunch by an experimental feeding machine. Chaplin depicted what anyone could see: There are human limits to speed and efficiency.

The twentieth century would see the proliferation of fast food, of which the global restaurant chain McDonald's was the pioneer. To this point, in 1993, sociologist George Ritzer coined the term "McDonaldization" to refer to "the process by which the principles of the fast-food restaurant are coming to dominate more and more sectors of American society as well as the rest of the world."[45] The four principles that he identified—efficiency, calculability, predictability, and control—are not meant simply as a critique. As Weber before him, Ritzer recognizes the utter appeal and value of these principles for task accomplishment. As consumers, we also recognize and value the same. Their enduring draw for consumers is still evident today, as Ritzer acknowledges that McDonaldization could well be relabeled "Amazonization" because digital transactions only intensify the earlier principles that brought McDonald's to international acclaim and condemnation.

In certain communication contexts, we can also see how these transactional, limited frame, linear interactions can be valuable. As described in this chapter, everyday digital communication can be used fruitfully in this regard for routine, unambiguous communication. Similarly, for any number of reasons, selecting the chat option for customer service support might be a better option than the phone call. However, as the Safety Net and American football cases illustrate, fast communication design logics are insufficient as the *only* option as I elaborate in the Children's Advocacy Centers of Texas timescape.

4
Slow Logics: The Communication Theory of Going Slow to Go Fast

If you want to go fast, go alone.
If you want to go far, go together.

—West African proverb

Slow communication design logics are far from new. They are the original means of task accomplishment. For example, in the mid-twentieth century, cultural anthropologist Edward T. Hall described what he called "polychronic (P-time) cultures" and "monochronic (M-time) cultures." In the former, relationships were the primary means of task accomplishment. The slow CDL premise that communication has a nonlinear relationship with time, that it unfolds through multiple time frames, and that it is transcendent are evident throughout Hall's rich description of interactions and institutions in P-time cultures.[1] He observed how work was driven by temporality (instead of time) in these cultures: People responded to events and relationships as needed, in the moment. He called it "polychronic," meaning many things at once, because multiple processes, relationships, and events were engaged simultaneously. This approach was in stark contrast to what he called "monochronic cultures," first emergent during industrial capitalism. In M-time cultures, task accomplishment was driven by time (i.e., clocks and calendars) while temporal demands (i.e., process-based, event-based and relational needs) receded into the background. He called it "monochronic" because (prior to digital communication) it meant that people focused on one thing at a time, much as the hands of a clock tick incrementally forward in a linear fashion. In *The Dance of Life: The Other Dimension of Time*, Hall explains:

> Though M-time cultures tend to make a fetish out of (time) management, there are points at which M-time doesn't make as much sense as it might. Life in general is at times unpredictable; and who can tell exactly how long a particular client, patient, or set of transactions will take. These are imponderables in the chemistry of human transactions. What can be accomplished one day in ten minutes, may take twenty minutes on the next.[2]
>
> Some Americans associate schedules with reality, but M-time can alienate us from ourselves and from others by reducing context. It subtly influences how we think and perceive the world in segmented compartments. This is convenient in linear operations but disastrous in its effect on nonlinear creative tasks.[3]

He points to the linear, transactional, single-frame focus—consistent with fast communication design logics—that drives M-time. Although he observed M-time and P-time across national cultures in the last century (where M-time was predominant in parts of Europe and the United States, and P-time was predominant on the continent of Africa, across Mediterranean countries, in part of Asia, and in Arabic-speaking countries), Hall also observed that different task accomplishment paths exist across subcultures, domains of life, and even individuals.

In the twenty-first century, certain task-related differences that originally distinguished monochronic and polychronic cultures have become blurred. Of course, digital technologies now facilitate doing many things at once *precisely because of a time-based focus that excludes temporal processes.*[4] Nonetheless, Hall's description of poly-chronism points to the fundamental utility of relationships in getting things done. To better understand the idea of relationships as a means of task accomplishment from the perspective of chronemic design, consider that to accomplish any task *three interrelated questions about the task specifications* must be answered:

1. *What?* i.e., the contours of a "task" must become apparent
2. *How?* i.e., an approach or path that enables task accomplishment is determined
3. *Why?* i.e., a purpose focuses the work, acting as a filter regarding what tasks and processes will support or hinder its completion

Although both fast and slow CDLs are used in the service of time-sensitive task accomplishment, the answers to these three questions differ, as I elaborate using a well-known example from the high-tech industry: Agile methodology. It illustrates what it means for a task to be enabled by relationships and for the purpose of relationships—even when the work product itself is not relational in nature. I begin with it because it provides high-level answers to the what/how/why of task accomplishment from a slow communication design logic.

After the example of Agile, I deliberately slow down the rhythm in this chapter (by comparison to the rest of the book). Because slow CDLs have not been made visible or privileged in most organizations since the birth of the Industrial Revolution, I take my time describing one particular, exemplary timescape—the Children's Advocacy Centers of Texas—where both slow and fast CDLs are used in concert in remarkable fashion. The speed demanded by this complex work is not supported with the latest technologies, or corporate investments. Instead, an infrastructure that places relationships at the center of the organization drives task accomplishment. Therefore, I offer an extended description of this research setting.

Slow Communication Design Logics Underlying Agile Methodology

The Manifesto for Agile Software Development[5] exemplifies and helps to elaborate how and why relationships function as the primary means of task accomplishment in contemporary, complex, fast-paced work. Its principles perfectly reflect a slow communication design logic. Agile's founders were not communication designers or consultants, but their lived experiences in the field taught them to center relationships as the path rather than a detour to getting work done. The founders were a group of seventeen expert software practitioners—made up of programmers, developers, engineers, and scientists—representing a range of frameworks used in the software development industry (including Extreme Programming, SCRUM, DSDM, Adaptive Software Development, Crystal, Feature-Driven Development, and Pragmatic Programming). In 2001, they came together over one long weekend to discuss how to improve what they considered wrong with conventional approaches to software development.

The manifesto positions event-based, relationship-driven task accomplishment as fundamental to the speed (i.e., agility) proclaimed in its very name. Notably, it contains a simple list of values about how software development should proceed.[6] When viewed through a chronemic design lens, these values reflect four hypotheses about how communication best supports software development:

We are uncovering better ways of developing
software by doing it and helping others do it.
Through this work we have come to value:

Individuals and interactions over processes and tools
Working software over comprehensive documentation
Customer collaboration over contract negotiation
Responding to change over following a plan

> That is, while there is value in the items on
> the right, we value the items on the left more.

Viewed from the task lens of what/how/why, the central "what" of Agile is *working software* and *responding to change*. The "how" is through *customer collaboration* that relies upon *individuals and interactions*.

Next, the "why" is addressed at length in a series of twelve principles[7] that follow the manifesto. The first principle is that:

- Our highest priority is to *satisfy the customer* through early and continuous delivery of valuable software.

Thus, although the task is agile software development, customer satisfaction is the "why." That is, the clock-based aspect of timeliness is important because of its tie to relationships. The principles go on to underscore speed enabled by and in the service of relationships. Notably, this speed is achieved through focusing on temporality rather than time. Their task-based principles are decidedly temporal (italicized for emphasis) leaving room for interaction to be the driver of time-sensitive task completion:

- Deliver working software *frequently*, from a couple of weeks to a couple of months, with a *preference to the shorter timescale*.
- Welcome changing requirements, even late in development. *Agile processes harness change for the customer's competitive advantage.*
- *Working software* is the primary measure of progress.
- Agile processes promote *sustainable development*. The sponsors, developers, and users should be able to *maintain a constant pace indefinitely*.
- *Continuous attention* to technical excellence and good design enhances agility.
- Simplicity—the art of *maximizing the amount of work not done*—is essential.

What they go on to articulate about relationships is also contrary to the predominant fast communication design logics they sought to change in software development:

- Business people and developers *must work together daily* throughout the project.
- Build projects around motivated individuals. *Give them the environment and support they need, and trust them to get the job done.*
- The most efficient and effective method of conveying information to and within a development team is *face-to-face conversation*.
- The best architectures, requirements, and designs emerge from *self-organizing teams*.
- At regular intervals, *the team reflects on how to become more effective, then tunes and adjusts its behavior accordingly.*

The founders were clear that this view of relationships was far from conventional, so much so that they called themselves "organizational anarchists." As for the centrality of relationships, Jim Highsmith describes that "Agile Methodologists are really about 'mushy' stuff—about delivering good products to customers by operating in an environment that does more than talk about 'people as our most important asset' but actually 'acts' as if people were the most important, and lose the word 'asset.' So, in the final analysis, the meteoric rise of interest in—and sometimes tremendous criticism of—Agile Methodologies is about the mushy stuff of values and culture."[8] Indeed, in the two decades after its introduction by software development practitioners, the principles of Agile would become incredibly influential in the profession and later spread to domains outside of software development, including sales, customer service, the C-suite, human resources, project management, and operations.

The Agile theory of communication could be stated like this: "Individuals and interactions, working software, customer collaboration, and responding to change should drive software development."

It reflects the three elements of slow communication design logics as the most effective path toward Agile software development. First, the collaborative process needed for Agile to succeed depends upon considering multiple frames of interaction. It centers regular day-to-day interactions and works toward finding a sustainable long-term pace that is necessarily both forward thinking as well as reliant upon learning from the past. Second, it follows an inherently nonlinear trajectory. Self-organizing teams require that managers "give it time" to work without interference. This includes time to regularly reflect on how to do it better and adjust in response. Like the process of "zoom and focus" that I described in chapter 2, this reflexive process is needed to help them better understand the emerging timescape of a particular project. Third, the belief in interaction as the path to transcendence is implied in their focus on face-to-face conversation (as Kee's virtual teams described). It is reflected in their conviction that the "mushy stuff" is what allows for the delivery of excellent products to customers.

As Agile has grown and been introduced into more and more organizations, as often as it succeeds in one organization, it fails in another. This is because the design hypotheses upon which it rests are inconsistent with the fundamental theory of fast communication designed into many organizations.[9] Over time, industry professionals (including its founders) have lamented what has become of Agile when put into the wrong hands. Blog posts such as "Agile is Dead (Long Live Agility)"[10] and "Agile at 20: The Failed Rebellion"[11] point to the mismatch between the principles outlined in the manifesto and the organizational practices that get labeled (and billed) as Agile. They argue that it has become a meaningless marketing term with little or no resemblance to its core principles. What is worse, not only does it now regularly fail to produce better outcomes for this reason, but it is also misused to lead teams to longer work hours and set even more unrealistic goals for their work.[12] The idea of speed sells easily, but changing organizational cultures to embrace the nonlinear trajectories necessary for that speed is much more difficult. Embracing Agile relies upon accepting the reality of uncertainty and investing in relationships as the best way to manage it, both of which rely upon slow communication design logics.

Fast and Slow by Design: Complementary Theories in the Children's Advocacy Centers of Texas Timescape

In the same way that Agile methodology was designed to change conventional organizational practices around software development, the children's advocacy centers movement was designed to change long-held institutional practices around the treatment and prevention of child abuse. Until the late twentieth century, social service and criminal justice agencies worked child abuse cases in isolation rather than together, and the outcomes were predictably disastrous.[13] From an organizational, health, and public policy perspective, it was inefficient and dangerous. Different agencies learned about different aspects of the case and the information was rarely shared, making successful prosecution more difficult.[14]

The lack of communication among agencies and the fact that systems were overburdened meant that cases frequently went unaddressed altogether or received delayed attention. This led to protracted abuse and sometimes the death of children. Additionally, even for cases that were successfully prosecuted, the policies in place (and the lack thereof) created additional trauma for children and their families during the case investigation. Medical exams rarely followed proper guidelines, children had to repeat details of their abuse during multiple interviews (sometimes more than a dozen times), families had to travel to various facilities to receive help, and their long-term needs—including therapy and logistical support—were typically unaddressed.[15]

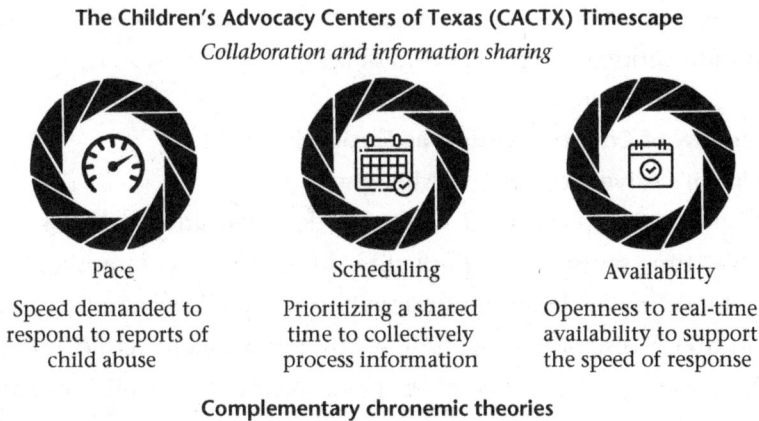

The Children's Advocacy Centers of Texas (CACTX) Timescape
Collaboration and information sharing

Pace	Scheduling	Availability
Speed demanded to respond to reports of child abuse	Prioritizing a shared time to collectively process information	Openness to real-time availability to support the speed of response

Complementary chronemic theories

Figure 4.1
The Children's Advocacy Centers of Texas timescape.

In the late 1980s, the CAC movement was born as a direct response to these catastrophic communication failures so common in child abuse cases around the globe.[16] The CAC movement offers a solution to these problems through providing infrastructure that supports the joint investigation of child abuse cases by multidisciplinary teams (MDTs). Globally, it has improved the speed of response and quality of collaboration across agencies. At its core, the movement leverages relationships for the purpose of task accomplishment—both directly and indirectly. Viewed from the task lens of what/how/why, their "what" is *collaboration and information sharing* across agencies and disciplines (i.e., MDTs). Their "how" is through building and maintaining *relationships*. Ultimately, *justice and healing for children and their families* (through victim support and advocacy) is their collective "why." In the following pages, I elaborate on the CAC intervention and how it uses both fast and slow communication design logics in a complementary fashion. Whereas in the last chapter I identified the problems with *inconsistent* and *competing* chronemic theories, the success of the CAC movement is due to its reliance upon *complementary* chronemic theories—a concept I introduced in the everyday digital communication example and will develop further here.

Overview of Communication-as-Design in the Children's Advocacy Centers Movement

As figure 4.2 depicts, local CACs are designed around MDTs that enable time-sensitive, high-quality interagency communication. The MDT model helps professionals from a wide variety of core child abuse disciplines—including law enforcement, child protective services (CPS), prosecution, medical, mental health, and the CAC itself (forensic interviewers, family advocates, mental health clinicians, and MDT coordination staff)—to work together to investigate, assess, prosecute, and intervene in cases of child abuse. These professionals are affiliated with or employed by local agencies that execute a formal written memorandum of understanding and MDT protocol that outlines both the commitment the agency is making and the specific protocols and procedures their staff will follow. CACs form partnerships with the following agencies: CPS, law enforcement, prosecution, medical (a local hospital, clinic, individual physician, and/or specially trained nurse), and mental health (therapist[s] with expertise in trauma-informed therapy modalities, who may be employees of the CAC or who may contract with the CAC).

Figure 4.2 illustrates the two layers of working a case: *information sharing* that relies upon fast communication design logics (i.e., leveraging information obtained from reports sent either from the statewide abuse hotline or 911) and *collaboration* that relies upon slow communication design logics (i.e., leveraging information obtained through face-to-face case reviews). First, the system of information sharing allows for the time-sensitive notification of all agencies. Next, collaboration through case reviews requires that agencies work closely together, which depends upon strong, collegial relationships. This is critical because the distinct and even conflicting occupational and institutional cultures that characterize law enforcement,

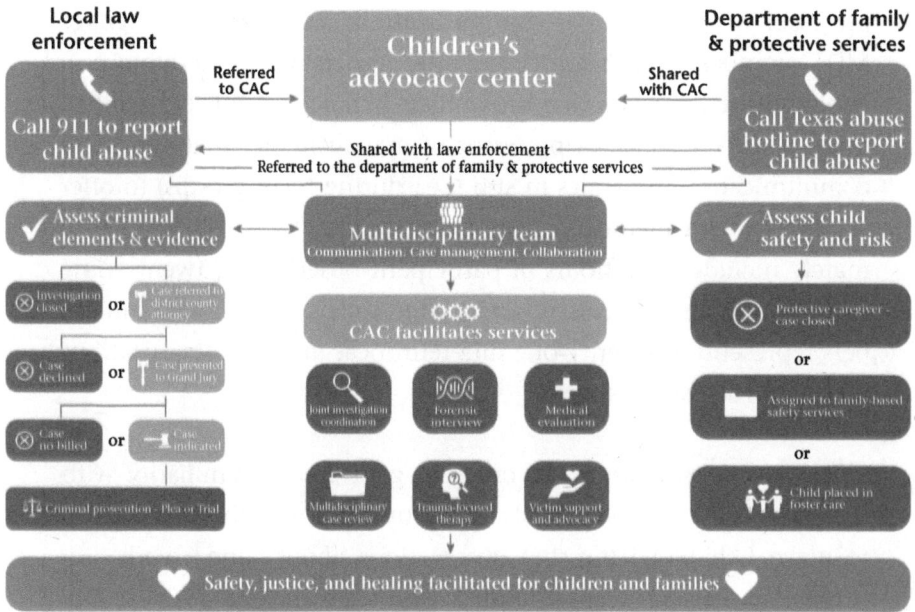

Figure 4.2
Flow chart for local children's advocacy centers (CAC).

prosecutors, therapists, doctors, nurses, and CPS communities must somehow come together in a cohesive, well-coordinated team. Case reviews are where they come together literally (in person) and figuratively (in terms of relationship building).

Data Collection: Learning About Communication-as-Design at the Children's Advocacy Centers of Texas

Our seven-person research team[17] collected data with the aim of highlighting existing practices associated with positive case outcomes across diverse CACTX member organizations throughout the state and identifying systemic barriers to effective collaboration and information sharing. Thus, to more fully understand the timescape of CACTX, from 2015 to 2017, we carried out a multiphase, multimethod, multidisciplinary investigation. To complement the broader chronemic analysis, one member of the team, Matthew McGlone, a professor of interpersonal communication, analyzed the language MDT members used in order to better understand underlying psycholinguistic processes that drove their behavior. Another member, Mary ("Mara") Waller, a professor of management, analyzed MDT communication dynamics in situ (i.e., during focus groups) to offer clarity on team members' shared experiences. Data collection ultimately included 217 hours of participant observation, twenty-nine focus groups and interviews, and a large-scale survey of 1,424 members representing seventy-one different local member organizations (i.e., CACs across the state).

Participant observation   In order to gain greater familiarity with the range of issues potentially faced by MDT members as well as to make field-based (on-site) observations about varied work processes, our research team attended seven case reviews at CACs representing urban, suburban, and rural populations. We also received CAC tours, before or after case reviews, to gain perspective about the various stages and logistic aspects of a case from the perspective of partner agencies, CAC staff, as well as children and their families. Additionally, we held weekly consultative meetings with executive leadership—either in person or by phone—for eighteen months (until the project "wind down"). Four of the MDT focus groups (described below) were conducted in person, which afforded us the opportunity to interact with the team in a field setting and observe firsthand a greater range of CACs. Relatedly, our team observed the MDT coordination staff trainings that occur regularly at CACTX headquarters and attended an organizational fundraiser at the invitation of CACTX to help us better understand the range of work they do and all of the stakeholders involved.

During our various on-site participant observations, we collected or reviewed any available MDT meeting agendas, coordinator training materials, and CAC outreach materials. We also studied the MDT training portal to review a greater range of training and reference materials and examined the CACTX website as well as local CAC websites. Additionally, as news stories were reported that featured local CACs, we also collected those.

Focus groups and interviews   We held twenty-seven focus groups. First, to hear from members in situ alongside others in their MDT, a total of seventeen MDT focus groups were held with established and ongoing MDTs (four urban, four midsize, five rural, and four suburban). The MDT sampling strived for theoretical variance, aiming for MDT groups with varied dynamics, histories, and trajectories.[18] "Grand-tour" questions were used to elicit the teammates' everyday experiences with the MDT model and to specifically explore their communication practices.[19] Follow-up questions were used for clarification and/or further elaboration. All group discussions were audiotaped and transcribed. This set of transcripts totaled 430 single-spaced pages of text.

In addition to focus groups with intact MDTs, we wanted to ensure that participants had every opportunity to share freely (and voice any negative views of the MDT) away from other members of their MDT. To achieve this, we held an additional ten focus groups where members were together with others in their occupation only: CPS, family advocates, forensic interviewers, law enforcement, medical professionals, mental health professionals, prosecutors, CAC executive directors, and MDT coordination staff (two focus groups were held with MDT coordination staff). Focus groups were held either via videoconference or teleconference, depending upon availability. All group discussions were audiotaped and transcribed. This set of transcripts totaled 196 single-spaced pages of text.

Two scheduled occupational focus groups—prosecutors and law enforcement—had multiple last-minute cancellations that resulted in only one person attending. As a result, we turned these scheduled focus groups into interviews. Similarly, one scheduled MDT meeting was canceled due to recent (disruptive) changes in partner agency roles. In place of the focus group, we conducted an interview with a senior member of the administration. We used an unstructured interview schedule given the unique (impromptu) nature of these three interviews.

Survey Based on emergent themes found in the focus groups and interviews, a questionnaire was designed and distributed to all MDT members across the seventy-one CACs in order to further explore the issues raised in the focus groups across the entire population of MDTs. Both descriptive and multivariate statistical analyses were used to analyze the questionnaire data, including frequency distributions, factor and reliability analyses, and mediation and multiple regression techniques. We used the Qualtrics survey tool to host an online questionnaire. We followed the Dillman Survey Methodology, including the use of a prenotice email announcing the survey, a launch email with the survey link, and two follow-up email reminders before we closed the survey link.[20] We distributed the survey to all seventy-one CACs, and sixty-eight of the CACs had MDT members who participated.

Respondents' tenure in their current position ranged from less than a year to thirty-nine years. Their demographic makeup was approximately two-thirds female (i.e., 38 percent male; 62 percent female), with ages ranging from twenty-one to seventy-six, and a range of ethnic/national backgrounds, with the majority of participants coming from White (71.1 percent) or Latino (21.4 percent) backgrounds. The remaining participants identified as Black (3.8 percent), Indigenous (0.9 percent), Asian/Pacific Islander (0.5 percent), and other (2.4 percent). A total of 1,424 people responded, which represents approximately 36 percent of the population to whom it was distributed—a strong response rate for online surveys of this type. Due to missing data from incomplete surveys, our final usable

Table 4.1
Survey participation frequency by MDT member type

MDT Member Type	*n*	%
Law enforcement	382	36.0
CPS	227	21.4
Prosecutor	88	8.3
Doctor	10	.9
Other	87	8.2
Nurse	31	2.9
Family advocate	68	6.4
Forensic interviewer	63	5.9
Clinical therapist	81	7.6
MDT coordination staff	24	2.3
Total	1,061	100.0

sample size was 1,061 for most statistical analyses. This represents an excellent sample size for all multivariate statistical analyses, improving the statistical power and reducing error. Table 4.1 reports the survey participation frequency by occupation.

Understanding the Design Features in the CACTX Timescape

#1:   What is the *communication process* that CACTX wishes to support? What are the accompanying messages (i.e., *theories of communication*) about how best to achieve it?

Collaboration and *information sharing* across multiple, independent agencies and professions are the two communication processes CACTX wishes to support through the two-layered MDT model (figure 4.2). Note that a given MDT is made up of dozens of people from different professions and multiple (often bureaucratic) agencies working together. Its power, its agency, and—ultimately—its speed

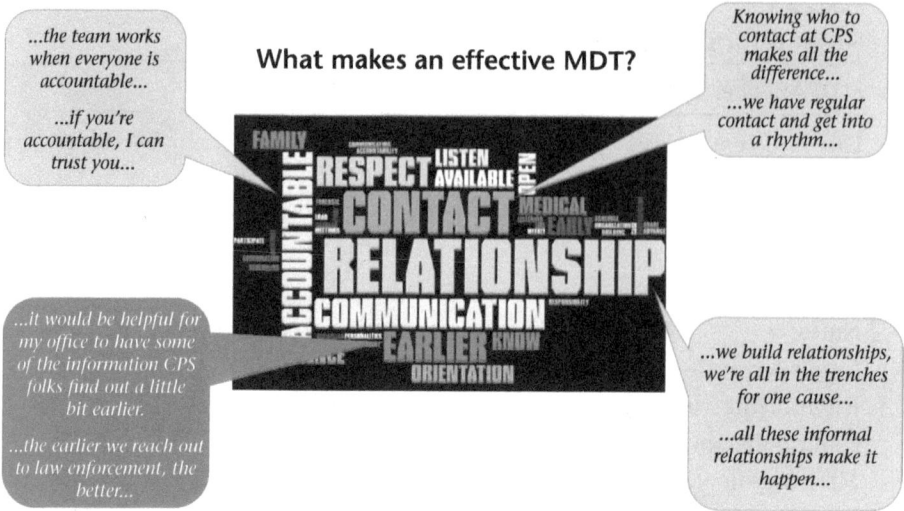

Figure 4.3
Word frequency cloud for MDT effectiveness.

stems from the relationships that members build. This is the "what" of CACTX—that is, relationships are the primary means of task accomplishment. It is what allows members to do their work (i.e., arrests, prosecutions, counselling, and prevention) because no one member agency can successfully do it alone. In our focus groups, we asked what makes an effective MDT. Figure 4.3 depicts the word-frequency cloud—an illustration of the most frequently used words to answer this question. The most common answer was relationships.

Each of the two communication-as-design interventions provided by CACTX supports the "how": (1) time-sensitive information sharing and (2) high-quality collaboration through the MDT case review. Of course, the "why" is the service that MDTs ultimately provide to children and their families. At its core, relationships are the work (the "what"). The "why" can be anything, but relationships are always the "what" in slow communication design. That's the job.

The overarching theory of communication that guides CACTX is *communicate slow to go fast.* This is realized through two distinct and complementary chronemic theories. One concerns the information sharing design intervention (i.e., CACTX receives abuse reports and quickly shares them with MDT member agencies). The guiding theory of communication regarding information sharing derives from fast communication design logics: *Member agencies should have rapid access to shared information in order to protect children.* With regard to the collaboration design intervention (i.e., CACTX provides infrastructure for the joint investigation of child abuse cases by MDTs), the guiding theory of communication derives from slow communication design logics: *Member agencies should participate in case reviews because a collaborative approach improves outcomes for children and their families.*

#2:   What is the *timescale* of this communication process?

Information sharing   In subjective terms, the timescale of the information sharing process can be characterized as immediate. In objective terms, it unfolds within a matter of hours. Each time a new case is reported, a series of notifications are put in place so that all member agencies receive the information as quickly as possible. It all begins here.

Collaboration   We discovered two types of MDT collaboration: formal (scheduled) and informal (real time). Thus, collaboration occurs over multiple timescales. Formal collaboration is designed to begin with the multidisciplinary case review, where each member provides case updates and receives information from other members. Reviews range from as often as weekly (in urban areas, or where member agencies are colocated in the same building) to every other month (in rural areas, due to the long distances MDT members must drive).

Beyond the scheduled reviews, we found that informal real-time collaboration occurs around-the-clock for many teams to supplement formal, scheduled interaction. As one MDT member (by the pseudonym of Joe) described:

It's not only a nine to five thing, because I don't know how many times I've texted [Medical] two or three o'clock in the morning, getting called out on something, and saying to Doc, "This kid has these injuries, what do you think?" and he texts me back or calls me at two or three o'clock in the morning [crosstalk 00:57:36]. Or I'll call [Forensic Interviewer] at two or three o'clock in the morning and say, "Hey, I need an interview now." And she makes it happen, so it's not just a nine to five thing. It's really a twenty-four-hours if needed and that's a blessing for us.

The need for this collaboration between case reviews became clearer as we better understood the timescale of each member's work (pictured in figure 4.4). In one of our early meetings with the executive leadership team, the function of the MDT model was described as traffic control for a six-lane highway. The various child abuse disciplines—law enforcement, district attorneys, medical, forensic interviewers, therapists, and family advocates—all occupy different lanes, speeding by at different times. They need a formal mechanism (i.e., the multidisciplinary case review) to monitor and direct their forward movement (including slowing it down at times) in order to avoid certain disaster.

Therefore, during the focus groups, we used a method called "time-lining."[21] We asked each member to visually recreate the timeline of their work on a case—from beginning to end.[22] Participants were then asked to draw the related lines of communication that took place during the case they depicted. This allowed us to see important chronemic differences across agencies. Although the timelines varied somewhat across members from the same discipline (because no two cases are the same), the type and timescale of communication across agencies highlighted why the case reviews were so critically important to developing a shared rhythm and relationship among member agencies. It also explained why the case reviews were supplemented with even more communication in real time.

Working across multiple timescales   Figure 4.4 includes illustrative examples of the timescale of members' information sharing

Forensic Interviewer Timeline

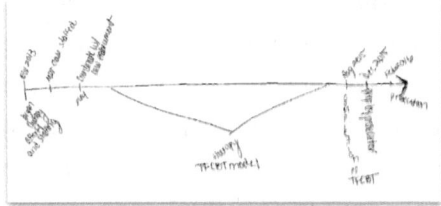

Mental Health (Therapist) Timeline

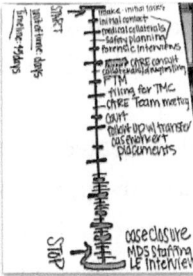

Child Protective Services Timeline

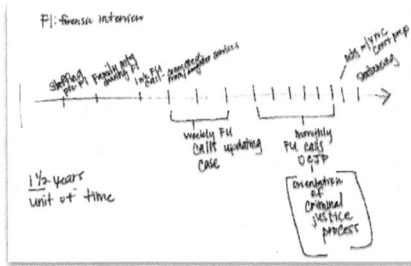

Family Advocate Timeline

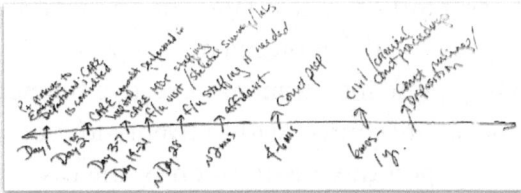

Medical (Physician and Nurse) Timeline

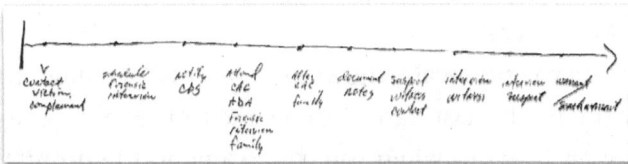

Law Enforcement Timeline

Figure 4.4
The timescale of cases across MDT member agencies.

and collaboration. At the smallest timescale, the *forensic interviewer* timeline was the only timeline constructed using minutes (rather than days) to indicate their involvement with the last case they completed. Although it was cut off in the fax machine they used to return it (i.e., this was a videoconference focus group), we can see that at minute 55, the interview began, and it ended by minute 58 for a total of three minutes. By the hour, the forensic interviewer had taken the child to another room and offered them a snack, and by five minutes after the hour, the forensic interviewer had already burned a DVD for the detective.

At the next timescale, the *CPS* professional indicated that their involvement in the last case they worked lasted approximately forty-five days. It began with an intake process prior to the forensic interview that occurred a few days later. The CPS professional then appeared in court and followed up with the transfer caseworker and placements. Almost forty-five days later, the case was closed, and an interview was given to law enforcement. The work of the CPS professional is tightly prescribed from an objective timescale perspective. They must initiate contact within twenty-four or seventy-two hours (depending upon the classification of the case) of receiving the report. Across multiple focus groups, we heard about how the CPS professional was the most overloaded and under-resourced of all of the MDT member agencies.

Moving up the timescale, the *medical* professional describes their involvement in the last case they worked on as taking approximately a year. It began when the child came to the hospital. After staffing and follow-ups, the physician gave a sworn affidavit two months later, was prepped for court four to six months later, and continued with the case until it received a court disposition.

The *family advocate* describes spending about eighteen months on their last case. Their involvement began during the staffing phase, which occurs right before the forensic interview. Next, they met with the family and followed up a week later to connect the mother and the daughter to appropriate services. They continued with weekly follow-up calls, then moved to monthly calls during the time that the family received an orientation to the criminal justice system. They stayed in contact with the family until sentencing eighteen months after their first meeting. Because their job is to begin with the family and stay in contact to assist them until sentencing, their work is framed by subjective timescales while also having regular objective touchstones driven by courts.

The *therapist* describes their last case as having taken three years. It started in November 2013 when the child began therapy after the forensic interview and staffing portion. The therapist then spent the first year coordinating with law enforcement. The child remained in therapy until late 2015. Months later, the therapist was prepped for court by the prosecutor, and the trial occurred in February 2016—three years after the case was opened.

While the forensic interviewer was the only member to recount their case in minutes, on the other end of the spectrum, the only MDT member to describe their work wholly in subjective timescale terms was *law enforcement*. The law enforcement timeline begins when they contact the complainant. This was followed by scheduling the forensic interview, contacting CPS, and attending an MDT case review. Note that they label this briefing as being with their "CAC family" (rather than the formal title of MDT) suggesting a particular tenor and tone of the review. Afterward, they go on to contact the suspect and witnesses, interview witnesses, interview the suspect, and get a search warrant. In contrast to CPS professionals who are typically expected to close a case within forty-five days, law enforcement has no objective time parameters regarding when they must close a case.

Ultimately, the multidisciplinary nature of the teams means that their time and temporality are distinct from one another. In many organizational settings, these differences lead to conflict,[23] but MDTs help to reduce the interagency barriers that give rise to it. In the next section, I elaborate on how the time-based practices surrounding the case review support the metaphorical traffic control it offers.

#3:   What *time-based assumptions and practices* support or obstruct this underlying communication process?

Multiple time-based practices support information sharing and the two layers of collaboration. In terms of information sharing, a fast, efficient *pace* achieves the speed needed to respond to each report of child abuse. In terms of formal collaboration, prioritizing *scheduling* allows members to slow down long enough to collectively process the information they receive. In terms of informal collaboration, an openness to real-time *availability* complements the efficiency of information sharing and the effectiveness of formal collaboration. As I mentioned earlier, each dimension of time is implicated in every setting, but I highlight these three to further explore how they are leveraged in a setting such as CACTX, where both fast and slow CDLs are used in a complementary fashion. Each one is elaborated, in turn, below. Several dimensions already discussed in other timescapes (*urgency*, *flexibility*, and *future*, especially) also emerged prominently for CACTX. So, I also point to the relationship among these varied time-based assumptions and practices in shaping communication-as-design.

The pace of information sharing crisis time   A critical design intervention associated with the children's advocacy centers movement is based on the sheer speed (or *pace*) of information, driven by a fast communication design logic. None of the other interventions matter unless a child is quickly afforded safety from abuse. Prior to the CAC movement, the ad hoc information sharing and coordination of members of various child abuse disciplines did not occur in a timely fashion. This is due to the tragic chronemic problems that typify large government-based social services agencies. Organizational members work in overburdened, underfunded systems so communication is anemic as a result. Not only is it delayed but it is often absent because the resources to respond to all the cases are severely lacking. Indeed, as a reminder of what is at stake in their work, many local CACs today are named after a child who died from abuse after multiple systems failed to respond in time.

Thus, driven by a fast CDL at the level of information sharing, for CACTX, communication begins with time (i.e., the notification). Communication processes must then fit into the time available (i.e., CPS has to make contact in as little as twenty-four hours, depending upon the report). The objective (not the content) of this first response is transactional. It all unfolds in a single frame of interaction (the present). And, importantly, communication costs time in this context. That is, the relationship between time and communication is linear. Efficiency reigns supreme in information sharing.

The scheduling of formal collaboration: Case reviews   Although the speed of information sharing is critical, the information alone is inadequate to make sure that it is acted upon in ways that lead to justice for all concerned. Therefore, the next step is to sit down and collectively discuss what to do with the information. This demands that members reserve and protect a regular place in their schedules. A forensic interviewer (by the pseudonym of Angela in a rural part of the state) explains why:

> For the rural we meet every other month. There's a couple of particular counties where the DAs just don't come. At one point one of them said he had more important things to do than to come to the meeting. It's just frustrating because then when it comes time to take this case to trial, if that even happens, and again, I'm only speaking of the rural areas, then they want to come talk to you or they want your help. But they've never met during the MDT to discuss with the team as a whole what was going to take place in terms of the case. Then along with that, sometimes even for court, they send you a subpoena and just expect you to be there and there's never any kind of pretrial meeting to talk about what it is that they need from me, the interviewer. . . . It makes it difficult for me, but most importantly, difficult for these victims and their families because they're left wondering. Often times they will talk to [the Family Advocate on

the MDT], the family advocate, and we'll have no answers for them because we don't know.

As Angela describes, the MDT engages in important work during case reviews that demands thoughtful participation from all members. It is not superfluous to working a case—it is essential to a strong case. Yet, participants told us that, from a strictly linear perspective, the case review feels counterintuitive on the surface: Why add one more thing to an already impossible schedule? Angela's example explicitly names these practical reasons, and it implies an additional symbolic one that is difficult to separate from the practicality of attending: It establishes and affirms your membership in a group. That is, beyond a simple coordinative tool, sociologist Eviatar Zerubavel explains that our schedules communicate solidarity with others.

Zerubavel describes how schedules are a design for temporal symmetry, a term he introduced and defined as temporal coordination that allows people to engage in the same activities at the same time.[24] This symmetry is used to symbolize one's affiliation with others. It also helps groups form, reaffirm, and deepen social bonds. Therefore, attending case reviews is more than a practical action, it is an implicitly social one. This function of case reviews was not in the intended design of the MDT model. Unlike Benedictine monks[25] who explicitly call out and celebrate the supernatural efficacy of temporal symmetry, for MDT members, it happens accidentally. Members told us that through talking aloud about their cases in a room with others who understand how difficult the work is, they receive much needed (and unexpected) social support that helps to manage *secondary trauma*[26]—that is, the adverse psychological effects of hearing about or witnessing the firsthand trauma experiences of another. During case briefings, participants inhabit a safe space to express their grief, horror, and anger. Members cry, curse, and use gallows humor. Early on, prior to our participant observation of a case briefing, the executive director of one CAC (by the pseudonym of Alex) sent the following caveat/orientation when we were arranging logistics by email:

> MDTs are an animal all their own and they operate in a nebula where they are accustomed to having privacy and space that belongs solely to them alone. My MDT particularly is irreverent, sometimes vulgar, competitive, biting, politically incorrect and often obnoxious but it is absolutely real. Our cases for February are particularly terrible (we had a DV homicide, a maternal suicide, and
> • a host of really difficult sex cases . . .) To do this work, and to do it as well as our team does, they have to be able to psychologically do whatever they must to get through it. I can't promise some of it might not be offensive.

The relational resources that were created by this temporal symmetry yielded professional and personal resources that were discussed at length across the MDTs in our study.

One consistent finding is that participants told us how belonging to a strong, cohesive MDT reduced turnover and managed burnout. For example, CPS has one of the highest turnover rates among the agencies, and one member from CPS (by the pseudonym of Sara) stated emphatically, "This team [MDT] is probably one of the biggest reasons why I haven't left CPS. It's because you come here, and you get the support that you don't have with the department, and they give it." These relational resources help members to continue in their jobs, decreasing turnover, which leads to greater team efficacy, better communication, and the improved institutional knowledge that comes from member longevity. Another CPS professional (by the pseudonym of Jamie) reflected, "I think any of us doing this work, you get burned out or discouraged at times, and generally whenever we go to [CAC location] everybody has a positive or encouraging attitude. At MDT meetings, we kind of cut loose and build each other up, or try to give each other advice." Similarly, a medical professional (by the pseudonym of Lar) described how the MDT helps to buffer her from the secondary trauma of her work:

From my perspective, that interaction and relationship with other members of the team are, in addition to doing the right thing for the children, are the reason I'm able to do my job and why I do this job. . . . I think we see this as a team effort and support one another in really difficult situations. I think that is essential to staying mentally healthy seeing these things on a frequent basis. . . . I think having other people that understand without a lot of facts, without having to explain much is why this job is doable. . . . I think having people like [Name] and [Name] and [Name] and all of the members of the MDT that do this on a daily basis, I really think that is a key to having a pretty successful career in this so you don't burn out quickly and have outlets for this.

These participants all describe the unexpected benefits gained from the relationships they form through attending case reviews: The common ground they share and deepen over time helps to manage the secondary trauma they all experience from working child abuse cases. In turn, their relationships help them to stay committed to an incredibly difficult career.

Their relationships with colleagues predicted not only their professional longevity but also their overall team performance. The results of our large-scale survey with 1,061 members from sixty-eight MDTs across the state suggest that simply making time for regular case reviews—showing up with other members of their MDT[27]—improves the day-to-day performance of the entire team. We found that more than half (53 percent) of the performance differences across MDTs could be attributed to how frequently MDT members attended case reviews.[28] Our analyses showed that this huge performance enhancement occurred because of what emerges through the case reviews. Specifically, attending case reviews improved communication, clarified roles, and built relationships. These communication outcomes then boost MDT performance. This was corroborated by what people told us in the focus groups. A prosecutor, by the pseudonym of Aaron, explained:

We usually have to have them interviewed in [County] county and I don't have really any rapport with any of those interviewers or anything like that and you got the gap and we never really see them in person during any meeting or anything. That makes it a lot more difficult. . . . I mean I know [Forensic Interviewer-1] and [Forensic Interviewer-2] very well. I think I've had them both testify for me. I've had [Forensic Interviewer-1] testify many times. When it's another interview in [County] county, I find them to be pretty professional but I just don't know them, I don't want to have any experience with them. I can't necessarily trust—just trust—their instincts on the field that they got with this particular child. I can't call them up and ask for some documents or whatever. I just don't have the same relationship so things move slower and just don't have as much confidence in whatever information they're giving me.

Ultimately, relational resources are inseparable from task resources. If we go back to the metaphor of the MDT model as traffic control for a six-lane highway, the speed that keeps all of the vehicles moving along is the quality of the relationships. An investigations supervisor, by the pseudonym of Cheryl, describes:

I can say six years ago when I came into investigations and learned about [City] Center, all of our agencies didn't work together like we do now. Law enforcement did their thing, we did our thing, prosecution did theirs. We didn't all have that communication. I think all of us have worked extremely hard, just in my six years, that it's one big case. It's not three separate ones. It's one case. That's how we run it. I can say I think it was a lack of communication six years ago coming in and people not knowing each other, and then us all working together to get to know each other and trust one another so we can have a solid case to send to [Prosecutor-1] or [Prosecutor-2].

MDT members' work exemplifies the meaning of transcendence. Showing up, making time in one's schedule to exchange information becomes far more than simply information sharing. It supports their performance at multiple levels, making the team more efficient and effective in ways they had not imagined. Given the fact that the work of each child abuse discipline follows a unique timeline (as figure 4.3 depicts), the case review becomes indispensable for saving time through leveraging relational resources. So, schedules can hold space for more than time. As I elaborate below, what began in these scheduled settings also expanded beyond this space and time.

Availability for informal, around-the-clock collaboration   Communication scholars Joshua Barbour, Rebecca Gill, and Kevin Barge contend that groups, organizations, and communities regularly intervene in their own communication through informal practices—a process they call "collective communication design." The MDTs we studied also described such a process that emerged over time through informal interaction. They told us that they developed norms of constant *availability* to bridge the gap between the two formal CAC interventions: the incredibly fast, yet context-free, information sharing that let members know a new case had been opened, and the slow, careful, and rich conversations that occurred at the table of the case review. Recall earlier that Joe described the timing of their work as "not only a nine to five thing." Therefore, they came to rely on the relational resources outside of the case reviews when they had to respond to an urgent issue. This led to the need for *flexibility* as a response to this experience of *urgency*.

This wide-ranging availability and the need for flexibility in response to urgent demands was framed by MDT members as a resource they can access because of their relationship. As an example, a CPS worker, by the pseudonym of Anita, shared:

> There are days where I have a schedule and then I'll get a call from someone saying, "Hey, we've got to interview this kid right now." So, I drop everything. And yes, it could be frustrating, but because we're flexible in nature with schedules. There are so many people with schedules, like in forensic, there's like three or four different instances that we need to be there, we have to be flexible. If it has to be after hours, it has to be after hours, we do what we need to do. And you just get it done. But because I have that relationship, we're okay, here especially.

Another member, by the pseudonym of Rori, positions this shared availability, flexibility, and urgency as unique based on the relationships in place. It doesn't work that way for everyone—it both draws from and, in turn, strengthens relationships:

> I did work in another jurisdiction for almost twenty years and being here, I think the difference for me in this MDT, is the sense of urgency is with the team and not just one entity saying I have an emergency and everybody else saying, well, your emergency is not my emergency. I think this team is really good about if someone says, "I have something that needs to happen today," the rest of the team members say, "Okay, then that's what we'll do." We come together.

Comments by a family advocate, by the pseudonym of Anna, underscore the tie between this informal communication-as-design and the rapport among MDT members:

> I haven't experienced not getting the cooperation or the support that I need whenever I'm calling anybody, care team, DA's office, CPS. I just don't have that experience where I haven't been able to get . . . Even the law enforcement officers that I've worked with don't work in the center, they're still out in the county. But they're still available to me, and the rapport that's developed, I'm always comfortable about even calling them.

Members supported informal collaboration through a combination of availability, flexibility, and urgency. Notably, they consistently highlighted how each of these time dimensions were tied to strong relationships. Members shared each other's sense of urgency, even when they weren't directly affected, a type of "referred" urgency. This led them to be flexible in order to respond to the other's needs. And, finally, it created norms and expectations of availability.

Although members expressed gratitude to each other for their availability, it was part of a work-around MDT members created to compensate for understaffing. Therefore, alongside their gratitude, we also heard about the pain and risks of persevering in large, bureaucratic government agencies that demanded so much and gave so little. A prosecutor, by the pseudonym of Sam, told us that his boss admonished, "It's not about how much resources you have.

That's just an excuse. It's what you're willing to dedicate your time to." Such sentiments are associated with a culture of personal sacrifice,[29] a dangerous substitute for material resources. Various news stories that emerged right before and during our fieldwork highlighted this danger. In one story, to compensate for the overburdened system in which they work, CPS workers started housing children on sofas in agency offices until they could find foster homes for them. Tragically, a fifteen-year-old girl being housed in the CPS offices left without supervision and was struck and killed by a van as she crossed the street. Clearly, their dedication to removing children from unsafe home environments was not enough. They needed adequate resources. This wasn't their failure. It was a systemic failure.

This failure points to the need for alignment between individuals and institutions, as it concerns slow communication design logics. Although CACTX is designed based on slow CDLs, its partnership is with agencies that operate from a fast CDL. The underfunded social services sector means that there are simply not enough people or resources to do the job effectively. The most committed organizational members are overworked as a result. As an assistant district attorney, by the pseudonym of Kate, reflected, "It's not necessarily any one investigator's fault. It's a systemic problem because they're overworked, they're underpaid. That's a whole big conversation." This systemic problem is the raison d'être for CACTX: to give agency members access to an infrastructure built on the slow communication design logics that compensates for the communication and staffing failures of these agencies. Nonetheless, because of the two competing design logics, MDT members face incongruity in their work. Their collective communication design that leverages time-based practices of availability and flexibility as well as the assumption of urgency often means taking heroic actions to meet the needs of children and their families. Yet, this heroism is not aided by their agencies. Instead, it amounts to organizational citizenship behavior, defined as "an individual behavior that is discretionary, not directly or explicitly recognized by the formal reward system, and that in the aggregate promotes the effective functioning of the organization."[30]

The problem for good organizational citizens within the local CACs that make up CACTX is the same fundamental problem for individuals caught between two design logics. Beyond the lack of external rewards, it puts them in a situation of overwork. They all described the intrinsic rewards of their work but, despite the utility of constant availability for the joint investigation and treatment of child abuse, it is also very stressful. A member of law enforcement, by the pseudonym of Tammy, explains flatly, "We're basically on twenty-four-hour call, seven days a week, because there's myself and my partner. There's two investigators in the whole county to handle all of these cases, okay?" A prosecutor in the Special Victims Unit of the District Attorney's Office, by the pseudonym of Drea, similarly expressed the overwhelm associated with her work: "The cases are so serious and so involved and there's so much at stake and I'm very emotional about all of it. So, you just don't feel like there's enough of you to go around or there's enough time to devote to these cases." Thus, when individuals operate from slow CDLs but work within institutions that operate from a fast CDL, the institution may reap rewards while the individual is overworked.

Reflecting on the Utility of Fast and Slow Communication Design Logics at CACTX

Through the complementarity between the efficiency of information sharing and the effectiveness of regular scheduling, MDT members adhered to and crafted a superb design of formal communication practices that led them to improved outcomes in the service of children and their families. This included a fast *pace* to support time-sensitive information sharing. It also included prioritizing *scheduling* to support members in slowing down long enough to mutually process and respond to the information they receive. Thus, the MDT model and the CAC movement is an excellent study in the complementarity of fast and slow communication design logics in the most time-sensitive and serious organizational settings.

MDTs also engaged in a process of collective communication design, wherein they developed informal norms of constant *availability*. This supported their ability to bridge the efficiency of information sharing in the form of reports that arrive daily with the effectiveness of collaboration with team members from other agencies. It speaks to their commitment to the work—above and beyond any formal rewards. Indeed, their availability was a form of organizational citizenship behavior. Therefore, although productive in many regards, I also saw the risks associated with this level of availability amid such staffing shortages. Clearly, no one should be on call twenty-four hours a day, seven days a week. This is unsustainable.

Thus, outside of the CAC infrastructure, MDTs faced a hostile environment in multiple respects. First, their work entailed high levels of secondary trauma. As one of the physicians, by the pseudonym of Taylor, described, "My husband's a physician. He's a surgeon. He's a cancer surgeon, so he sees a lot of sad cases and can listen sometimes, but even he doesn't understand this." Additionally, a forensic nurse, by the pseudonym of Jane, depicted the gravity of what they might face even when they do their best:

> I think looking back over the last year for 2015, we had a lot of death cases. And in one particular death case, there was a lot of people from the MDT team that were involved. And we worked really well together, and when we went to the MDT meeting, I believe it was Susan that had made a point to say, "We understand that you guys are tired, that you have been through a lot this week and we share your frustration, your concern." I think just taking that effort to acknowledge that we all equally were tired and exhausted and emotionally drained. I think that really meant a lot, at least for me.

Therefore, alongside the relationships they forge that allow them to persevere, they experience incredibly difficult work. This difficulty suggests that slow CDLs are not simply a luxury that only well-resourced, relaxed professionals with low-stakes jobs can afford to use in their communication. Rather, the direr the setting, the greater the need for an organization and its members.

Second, in addition to engaging in a very traumatic work setting, key members are also employed by severely underfunded government agencies. As Kate said, and public records confirm, they are underpaid and overworked. This leads to a high level of turnover, which is a threat to each MDT. Tammy, who earlier talked about being on call 24-7 explained:

> I know when I worked in [Large City], one of the big issues with CPS was their lifetime as a case worker was averaging about six months. . . . Because you'd have to try to find out what's going on with the case and it's maybe three months later. Well, that case worker is gone and there's a new one reassigned, and they're just training. And a lot of times you couldn't get a hold of them because they were always in training. By the time they got out of that and they were working the field, they realized, "I'm moving on," so you've got a new case worker. Literally, six months was about the average. In [Other Large City], it was about five months.

Speaking to what that means for an MDT, a forensic interviewer by the pseudonym of Raye elaborated: "Any time there's any type of turnover or new people, it's a little bit of a learning curve for them to figure out where they fit in and get up and running and everything." Participants told us that their ongoing, long-term relationships provided stability amid the turnover. Essentially, their relationships not only helped them to do their job in material and emotional ways but also acted as a buffer to support the longevity of the institution.

Finally, I want to underscore just how remarkable it is that these professionals show up in the numbers in which they do. In addition to the secondary trauma, overwork, under-compensation, and high levels of turnover described above, many MDT members do not even have the support of their supervisors to attend case briefings. I first mentioned the concept of organizational citizenship behavior with regard to the collective communication design around availability. But this is their foremost good citizenship behavior: Agency participation is completely voluntary. An MDT member from the sheriff's office, by the pseudonym of Tori, shares: "Sergeant-wise, they either care or they don't. If they're not buying into it, I'm not stopped from coming, but if there was an issue, or I have something else to do, it's 'Don't worry about it, do what you need to do, that's a waste.' . . . I certainly don't get in trouble for not going." A forensic interviewer and family advocate, by the pseudonym of Kris, elaborates why members don't get the support from their supervisors:

> I don't think the people higher up actually understand the whole concept, and how important it is. Whether they've never dealt with it, or whether they've been too far removed from it for too long, or whatever it is, they make decisions based on not trying to hurt the team, but what they think is more priority than the team. I think they don't understand sometimes that this is really important, because a lot of stuff can get done here, and work can get done. Sometimes, it just takes a reminder to these bosses that this is important. Sometimes it doesn't matter what you do, they're not going to change their mind.

The mixed or missing support to attend case reviews reflects the competing chronemic designs of the MDT model (that operates through slow CDLs) and government-based agency work (that operates through fast CDLs).

Despite the disincentives to participate, members find the collaboration so essential for their work that they attend anyway. Members describe the transcendent nature of communication that unfolds. A detective, by the pseudonym of Joe, elaborates:

> A lot of times, we can get valuable information. . . . I mean so much so I get so much information in here that even if I don't have a case

on our weekly, I come down anyway just because I want to hear what everybody else's working. There's times that Jim's had a case up there, had I not come down here and heard what his case was, due to the discussion, you know what? As a matter of fact, this is in [City]. Although we're not all excited to hear those things when we get down here, they're vitally important because it knocks off a day or 2 of having to wait for another report and we can go and get started on things.

A forensic interviewer, by the pseudonym of Mary, echoes this transcendence, the experience of communication leading to unexpected and expansive outcomes:

> We mentioned before, we have a few law enforcement agencies that don't typically show up. They bring cases for interviews, and it's almost like a catch-22. I think some of them still don't have total buy-in to, you come here and you share information, because that's what we're doing. By not . . . I think if they were to come and keep experiencing it, they would see and feel the benefits of what happens here when you do that. By not doing that, it is a catch-22. It's like, 'Come and experience it,' but they don't want to come experience it.

Slow communication design logics guide this collaboration, as reflected in the three foundational elements. First, their interaction unfolds over multiple time frames, given the shared past and futures that come together in the case briefings. Second, the design reflects a nonlinear relationship between communication and time. Members attend case reviews (despite its counterintuitive nature) because it saves them time. Third, what unfolds is described as transcendent—unknowable and invaluable.

In conclusion, the MDTs we studied through the Children's Advocacy Centers of Texas demonstrated the extraordinary value of slow communication design logics to ultimately speed work and save time. Their timescape exemplifies how relationships are used to accomplish time-sensitive, incredibly urgent, and important tasks. That so many members voluntarily participate—despite the stark situations they face and the inadequate resources from which they draw—speaks to the distinctive power of slow CDL. The CAC movement has built an incredible infrastructure that has vastly improved the outcomes for child abuse across thirty-three nations and more than a thousand cities in the United States alone. Our own findings, drawn from survey and focus group data, corroborate existing research showing how the slow CDL associated with formal, regular collaboration leads to better child and family outcomes (including a higher conviction rate).[31]

5
Beyond Words: Signposts for New Timescapes

Don't get stuck on the level of words. . . . It's an abstraction.
Not unlike a signpost, it points beyond itself.

—Eckhart Tolle

In the opening pages of this book, I defined time as a symbolic marker that points toward the temporal but often hides it instead. This is what words and other symbols do.[1] Eckhart Tolle points to this in the quote above from *The Power of Now* as he explains present-moment awareness. It is an achievable state, but words alone are an insufficient guide and may even be misleading. This is also a challenge for the concept of fast and slow communication design logics. Therefore, before concluding the book in the next chapter, I want to pause here and clarify.

I am aware that the terms "fast" and "slow" may initially hide what I hope to convey. Slow is a misnomer. Fast is as well. Indeed, my intention in adopting them is to trigger the various contradictions and inaccuracies in our use of these words to allow us simply to begin again with the very (often polarizing) concepts at the heart of production in industrial and postindustrial culture. My objective throughout *Time by Design* is for us to reconsider how effective time-sensitive organizing unfolds and what it requires of our communication norms and practices.

I began in chapter 1 by establishing that all times are designed. I showed how time is a social technology, or tool, that we continually design and redesign in order to coordinate (and communicate) more easily with others. We use time in an attempt to standardize, homogenize, and regularize human temporality. The problem is that human temporality is inherently differentiated, heterogeneous, and slightly irregular. Therefore, good design considers the nature of the relationship between time and temporality. In the case of slow CDLs, temporality takes the lead, and time is designed to include it. In the case of fast CDLs, time takes the lead, and whether the temporal is included or excluded is not related to the primary goal of interaction. Understanding when each of these approaches is most appropriate for the communication demands faced by a group or organization is the focus of chapter 2. To that end, I introduced several concepts (i.e., timescale, time-based assumptions and practices, and timescape) and related questions that serve as design tools. Then, in chapters 3 and 4, I offered case studies that show more and less effective uses of slow and fast CDLs.

I shared case studies of communication-as-design that highlight where fast CDLs win—that is, in situations that are transactional by nature, that need only attend to one time frame, and where less communication saves time in the long run. I also showed where fast CDLs fail to provide the speed they promise when used in inappropriate settings. These case studies showed how a fast CDL fails by only attending to immediate short-term needs in settings where longer-term needs are also important, how it forestalls relationship development where it could transcend externally imposed limits, and how it adds considerable time to work by eventually requiring time for solving the problems it creates. In contrast, I offered examples and an extended case study that highlights the extraordinary power of slow CDLs. Now, in chapter 5, I offer some additional guidance and clarity about the process of chronemic design, especially using slow communication design logics.

Moving beyond the labels ("fast" and "slow") to the norms and practices toward which they point requires what designers Harold G. Nelson and Erik Stolterman call the "design way." The design way is driven neither by science nor art. It is also not found somewhere halfway between the two. Instead:

> Design is a third culture with its own founding postulates and axioms, with its own approach to learning and inquiry. Design is inclusive of things found in science such as reason and in the arts such as creativity. But just as science is inclusive of creativity it does not follow that science is the same as art or that art is subsumed under science. They are different ways of approaching and being in the world. This is also the case for design.[2]

They go on to argue that design encompasses the true (i.e., facts), the ideal (i.e., desires), and the real (i.e., the singular design that is brought into being). It relies upon wisdom and requires the ability to cope with uncertainty as one works to achieve the true, ideal, and real. It calls for leadership, and the resulting design is more than functional or efficient—it bears soul.[3] It relates holistically to its environment rather than existing in an isolated, remote relationship to it. Consequently, it moves people and changes them.

Therefore, in further support of cultivating this essential design wisdom, in this chapter, I want to sharpen and underscore three observations contained elsewhere in this book. Each signpost directs us beyond the words "fast" and "slow" to inherent qualities of the timescapes at which they point.

1. First, recognize that poorly run organizations give "slow" a bad name, confusing slow with nonresponsive, sluggish communication.

2. Next, in order to be effective, chronemic design must point to a complementary theory of communication.

3. Finally, a design culture is crucial to overcoming dominant cultural biases regarding fast and slow.

1. Poorly Run Organizations Give "Slow" a Bad Name

Fast communication design logics are used for everything in conventional organizational timescapes, regardless of fit. Accordingly, their spectacular failure is our predominant experience of communication in groups and organizations. We do not understand that it is a misused communication design logic—not communication—slowing us down. As a result, human interaction seems to be the gunk stuck in the gears of efficiency that ruins our perfectly designed engine. This is dangerous because it gives communication a bad (and undeserved) reputation, despite the fact that our most important institutions rely upon privileging communication: our legal system, our government, our educational system, our health-care system, and many more. Because people and communities and their interests are at the heart of these systems, it is critical that we recognize communication as at the heart of their transcendence, their way of learning from the past to build a better future, and their way of building long-term effectiveness into the way our institutions work. Therefore, slow CDLs are not just useful. Rather, recognition of their importance is vital to the most fundamental work in society.

However, not all communication-as-design is intended to support timely progress. In contrast with slow communication design logics, other design logics are meant to slow down, or even stop, communication. For example, delay tactics[4] are deliberately used by individuals, groups, organizations, and governments to accomplish a variety of goals.[5] In these instances, no attempts or assurances are made with regard to time-sensitive action. Organizational leaders and members are resigned to constant delay and deferment. In these cases, customers, clients, and organizational members are made to wait, and work is delayed because of broken systems and a lack of adequate resources.[6]

However, neither intentional delay nor resigned indifference reflect slow communication design logics. These chronemic strategies and outcomes, and others not explicitly described in this book, are in different categories altogether. For instance, delay tactics may be used in the service of what communication scholar Barbara O'Keefe describes as a "rhetorical design logic"—that is, formed on the premise that "communication is the creation and negotiation of social selves and situations."[7] Delay tactics may also be used in the service of what designer Carl DiSalvo terms "adversarial design"—that is, a type of design that evokes and engages political issues.[8] Both delay tactics and resigned indifference may involve the slowing of communication, but neither contains the three capacity-building elements— cultivating multiple time frames, nonlinear trajectories between time and communication, and transcendence—that are used in the service of time-sensitive interaction.

So, a variety of poorly designed or strategically designed interactions give "slow" a bad name. Although this book illustrates the power of slow, colloquially we tend to equate poorly run organizations and institutions with slow. We tend to think of being asked to spend lots of time that goes nowhere as slow. We tend to think of clueless, insular organizations as slow. We may even have images of corrupt, unresponsive, and sluggish communication as slow. To be clear, these are examples of wasteful, inefficient, and even unethical communication. In contrast, slow CDLs are respectful, even reverent, of the time and intellectual resources individuals invest to improve communication and work.

The reverence with which slow logics treat the time that people spend engaged with one another is exemplified by a consulting practice I observed decades ago. When I was in graduate school working on my doctorate, I had the opportunity to assist my dissertation advisor, David Seibold, with his consulting and training work for several organizations. Dave is internationally renowned for his research on organizational and team communication and a highly sought-after consultant for the same. He had been hired by an organization to help resolve internal team dynamics. During his first meeting with the team, I watched Dave convey a bold commitment that he made a condition of the work they would do together. He acknowledged that he was going to be asking a lot of the team—in terms of time as well as intellectual and emotional labor. He assured the team members that their engagement in the arduous process of change making would be worth it because management had agreed in advance to instituting whatever changes the team arrived at mutually. When he shared these parameters, I still remember the powerful shift that occurred in the room as members opened up, visibly relaxed, and engaged.

It is important to acknowledge this cultural baggage at the beginning of any design intervention that initially asks more of members' communication. In all of the organizational work I have done since that time, I regularly find at least one member (if not more) who is initially suspicious about being asked to participate. This is for good reason. Not only are the words that organizational members share to improve their work often ignored, sometimes these words are used against them. Its reality as a cultural expectation is depicted in the movie and cult classic *Office Space* in which employees are fired based on their (and their colleagues') open communication.

Even in nonwork settings, this experience is common. Civic engagement is often rewarded by months or years of time invested in community organizing that is completely ignored by municipalities. I was reminded of this while writing this book. I was hesitant to engage in an important issue for my neighborhood, given the other projects that demanded my attention. Nonetheless, my belief in the value of communication won out over my assumptive time scarcity. Neighbors spent weeks and then months working together—talking in person, over Zoom, via text, drafting letters, and attending the city's planning commission meetings that regularly lasted six hours and often went on even longer. When our concerns about the safety of children walking to and from school on an increasingly crowded street lost out to the interests of a large developer, members of the commission never explained their reasons. They even apologized to the developer for having to spend time talking about the issue without acknowledging residents' extensive unpaid participation in a process formally designed to engage the community. These inconsistent chronemic theories—declaring the value of community engagement without actually engaging the community—kill participation. A neighbor who declined to participate had foreshadowed this experience. He mentioned years of community engagement (that I saw him invest) met without change or explanation. So, this is the context that designers must acknowledge.

Notably, Dave's standard practice in team interventions reflected all three elements of slow communication design logics. He knew that most people carry with them past experiences of being asked to spend time engaging in problem solving (and communicating) that are simply overlooked if management finds their solutions inconvenient or costly in some way. Therefore, he acknowledged this "shared" past (i.e., an unfortunately common experience) to create a truly shared future that they were asked to shape together in the present. He also described the path of their work together as nonlinear (although not using this term), pointing out that it would take a lot of time and commitment up front but that it would ultimately address problems that had been preventing them from working together effectively. Finally, Dave did all of this because he knew firsthand—from his research and time in the field helping teams and organizations—that this sort of shared work is transcendent. It not only solves problems but also allows people to experience the best of what it means to be human in relationship with others.

2. Chronemic Design Must Point to a Complementary Theory of Communication

In contrast to the leaders who sought out (and agreed to) Dave's expertise, in other settings, leadership may see interaction as transactional, wasteful, and of limited utility beyond accomplishing short-term goals. This is the received view of communication based on industrial-era theories. In these cases, even if the organization or institution is designed for slow communication at a structural or even policy level—as it was with the planning commission above—it will not be realized in practice. In the last chapter, I described how this was the primary threat to MDTs and the children's advocacy centers. Their design was impeccable, but organizational leadership at the public service agencies they supported determined whether they were allowed to function as designed. This is why chronemic design must signify a complementary theory of communication in order to effect change.

Recall that theories of communication form the basic building blocks of any communication-as-design effort, and they reflect our beliefs about how interaction *should* function to shape our worlds. So, our experience of organizing is as much about what theories participants bring with them to interaction as it is about what communication affordances are built into the design. Although the structural changes afforded by design features are important, they are insufficient on their own. Without integrity, trust, and mutual respect among people in these organizations and institutions, slow communication design logics are not enough.

In earlier chapters, I referenced the classical school of management (that drove the Industrial Revolution), wherein the theory of communication is that human interaction is nothing more than a way of transmitting information. As a result, the associated communication-as-design focuses on limiting communication because of the time it takes away from what is seen as the real business of work: task accomplishment. Relatedly, I shared an excerpt from Taylor's *Scientific Management*[9] to give a flavor of how this method was deployed in the field. Managers used coercion, threats, and insults as supervisory tools to motivate work. Unsurprisingly, this was not well received by those they hoped to motivate. This approach was not only ineffective but also led to resistance at multiple levels. This resistance ranged from *malicious obedience* (following work guidelines to the "letter of the law," knowing that said guidelines would be disastrous when followed without their own intellectual labor) to *rate busting* (keeping production down through shared agreements with their colleagues) to outright *corporate sabotage*. Beyond these forms of resistance at the individual and team levels, it also led to union organizing, which was perhaps most feared by owners.[10]

Seeing the weaknesses of the classical school of management created the appetite for an alternative approach, but it did not change the underlying theories of communication that industry titans, consultants, and managers held. Instead, these bona fide classical school theorists simply shifted from using coercion and threats to positive reinforcement and incentives. It was called the "human relations school of management," and the changes were all superficial. Of course, employees saw through the lack of consistency and the empty words. So, it had limited utility. This is because the same theories of communication abounded, even if the tactics to extract more value out of employees were different. Unsurprisingly, none of it delivered any real or lasting change.

The failure of the human relations school is predicted by Nelson and Stolterman's argument that design requires attention to more than policy or structure. The human relations school amounted to no more than scientific management by a different name. It only attended to work from a scientific, or fact-based, approach. It neglected the "ideal" because of limiting theories of communication that could not envision workplace relationships beyond transactional communication, linear trajectories, and the present time frame. This offers caution to groups and organizations wanting to redesign work around slow communication design logics. Without the interrelated relational principles (i.e., the ideals) of transcendence, nonlinearity, and multiple time frames, the outcome will be a set of rules and guidelines that no one uses in their daily interaction.

The American educational system has been critiqued for this same shortcoming.[11] School districts regularly trumpet the latest educational theories to change the world. They recruit and hire inspired individuals to make it happen through attending to the "whole student."[12] Yet, when these teachers arrive, they find that test scores and discipline rule the day. Historian and education scholar Joel Spring describes that this is because the origin of public schools was to create a well-behaved working class. Therefore, the underlying theory of communication that drives school-based interaction is one of communication as a tool to effect behavioral reform and vocational readiness.

A theory centered on behavioral reform and vocational readiness is in conflict with the slow communication design logics needed to attend to the whole student. For instance, not only are nonlinear trajectories between time and interaction inefficient to manage, but also transcendence as a goal of communication certainly does not foster the conformity of thought needed for the more limited goals that Spring describes. Similarly, attending to multiple frames of interaction—not limited to skills placement and test preparation but in relation to the whole student—is simply not possible with the resources given and the demands asked. Of course, some remarkable individuals persist, despite the structures afforded them. These are the teachers whom we remember, whom we visit, whom we maintain relationships with throughout our lives. However, many others, like the CPS workers I described in chapter 4, will soon leave the profession already burned out and disillusioned. Notably, in the Great Resignation, the number of teachers quitting between January and November 2021 rose 148 percent above the pre-pandemic level (e.g., compared to 27 percent in the retail sector).[13]

The literature on work–life balance policies and digital communication technologies also illustrates how major organizational innovations face a similar lack of complementarity.[14] For example, a former student of mine and his spouse (a director-level executive at a national retail establishment—I'll call him Stew) once took me on a tour of their national headquarters. At one point in the tour, as we were overlooking the scenic downtown view, the window coverings started to automatically close, and the lights began to dim. Stew casually walked over to a panel on the wall, input a code, and the place came back to life. The lights brightened, and the shades receded. He explained that the organization had designed the offices to physically shut down at 5:00 p.m. to get employees to go home and live out the "work–life balance" policies that the company advertised. He went on to say that they never go home at that time. They routinely work hours after that mythical time when the building is designed to shut down. In fact, they did this workaround on a daily basis so the design was completely ineffectual. Worse, it reminded employees of the lack of consistency between the policies and the true job expectations. The reality was that their expected workload could not be accomplished within the mythical time designed into the building.

Put differently, the executive's formal (i.e., written and advertised) "ideal" did not comport with the "truth" (i.e., the daily actions and activities of organizational members). The design was an attempt to bend one or the other so that they would meet, but this required either reducing the workload or being honest about the demands they were asking of employees. I learned that the company had changed ownership not long before. The design was material evidence of the conflict between the old culture (that was widely known and respected in the industry for holding presumptions about communication that reflected a slow logic) and the new culture (that was conventionally fast). Stew did not stay with the company for much longer, and I will add that its national reputation for extraordinary customer service noticeably declined under the new ownership.

To summarize this second point, then, slow communication design logics must be accompanied by complementary theories of communication. There is no masking cynical views of communication and short-term value propositions with either internal or external stakeholders. As people instinctively understood the human relations school as manipulative and empty, the same will hold true for any communication-as-design that is not coherent and whole. For example, the focus on relationships as a means of task completion should not be confused with an extraction model. That is, the idea of using a relationship to extract something particular from a person (in colloquial terms, "using" them) is not consistent with a slow CDL. That would be a transactional relationship. Rather, the transcendence associated with a slow CDL presumes that everyone potentially has something to offer, and what that something is or when it will be relevant cannot be known in advance.

Failure to recognize the transcendent quality of relationships can be costly, as the developer I mentioned in the previous section discovered soon after winning the city's planning commission hearing. Although they "won" in terms of receiving approval by the city, they ultimately lost out economically and never began the project. It turns out that as they proceeded, they realized it wasn't practically feasible. This concern was publicly shared with the developer by more than one member of our neighborhood on more than one occasion. The first time I heard it was during a formal meeting—requested by the neighborhood—so that we could learn more about their plans. During the meeting, it became obvious to everyone that the developers weren't interested in anything we had to say. They didn't ask questions and didn't listen to what was shared. After all, what could we know that they didn't? They attended for the same reason that managers from the human relations school use the equivalent of employee suggestion or customer suggestion boxes—it looks good. They wanted to be able to report to the planning commission that they met with us because, like suggestion boxes, "open communication" is often exploited as a stand-in for relationship building. But you can't fake a belief in transcendence by simply holding a listening session.

In the absence of a belief that interaction is transcendent, organizational members are hurried along by checking boxes and plowing forward in the single-minded pursuit of speed. This can lead to mistakes as well as wasted time and resources.[15] In reality, the developer would have saved time and money by slowing down and engaging with us in good faith for the thirty-minute Zoom call. Making room for transcendent, rather than transactional, interaction reflects the practice of design wisdom, elaborated in the next section.

3.   A Design Culture Is Crucial to Leveraging Slow Communication Design Logics

In addition to considering the prevailing theories of communication, there is the related issue of cultural beliefs around time. Although time is mutually constituted with communication (as I illustrated in chapter 1), it also merits close attention on its own. Cultural anthropologist Edward T. Hall, mentioned in chapter 4, described time as part of the *core* level of culture.[16] As such, it resides at the most basic level of our beliefs. These beliefs are so fundamental that they are hidden, even from ourselves. Rather than being aware that we hold certain beliefs (which would effectively mean that other beliefs are possible), we view our beliefs as truths. This precludes openness to other beliefs about time.

What does this mean, then, for adopting an unconventional design approach toward time such as represented by the slow CDLs described in this book? An approach that is decidedly off-brand in contemporary Western culture? It underscores the necessity of a design culture and its accompanying wisdom. A design culture must be cultivated in order to make change. Design thinking supports groups and organizations in moving beyond cultural beliefs that limit what is possible. It was what led to the CAC movement. These organizations faced unspeakable horrors if they continued on the same path. They knew the facts and held the desire for change. Yet, alone, neither was adequate. It was the design itself that changed others' ideas about what was possible. Over and over, professionals told us that they thought it would be a useless waste of time until they experienced it firsthand. Nelson and Stolterman explain, "Functionality, efficiency, cleverness, usefulness, or whatever other pragmatic measurement we can come up with, doesn't capture, in totality, the way people relate to a design." Instead,

> The meaning and value of a design is taken in as a feeling of being deeply moved and, as a consequence, of being significantly and meaningfully changed. When we encounter a design's essence or soul, our basic assumptions and worldviews are most likely to be challenged. Something profound happens to us as a consequence of our encountering a design at the level of its ensoulment. Our understanding of the world, of our own place in it and our core judgments, all are changed.[17]

This description draws from psychologist James Hillman's argument that all cultural, social, and physical environments are conveyors of soul.[18] Cultures can resist change for long periods, but eventually, they will face internal and/or external pressure to change. In those historic moments calling for change, the cultures that have successfully managed these crises have done so through a radical transformation that is consistent with design wisdom.

Nelson and Stolterman argue that design wisdom is the first tradition of humankind, our natural inheritance as human beings. Across epochs, however, it has been supplanted by reductive thinking in Western society, eroding the values of a design culture in the process.[19] Now, to navigate the major changes experienced in the twenty-first century, design wisdom is needed to infuse the analog into the digital. An analog approach reflects design thinking. It is holistic and complex, unable to separate parts into discrete and isolated fragments. In contrast, a digital approach reflects reductive thinking. It is focused on dividing the whole into even, undifferentiated parts. As a prototypical example of digital thinking, Nelson and Stolterman offer "the division of the day into hours, minutes, and seconds that are indifferent to the particular qualities of any one day."[20] It mirrors the critique expressed through Makonnen's *Rock Standard Time (RST)*. While time-driven design is digital, temporally driven design is inherently analog. Hence, design wisdom can only be accomplished through attention to temporality (i.e., the analog) rather than time alone (i.e., the digital). Understanding the place of both (analog/temporal and digital/time) and how they work together to focus human activity reflects design wisdom.

Anyone who lives in an extreme geographical climate, such as Austin, Texas, where I live, can sense the inherently analog qualities of the "day." The summers are incredibly hot. So, every minute of the day is not the same. They are not all equally well suited for outdoor activities, and this helps residents and tourists alike to focus their attention and activities. Instead, every minute of the day has its own agency, or power, to include and exclude a range of interrelated behaviors. The power is not absolute, of course—like an on-time commercial flight or a movie start time—but it certainly influences what many people want to do at particular times. A digital clock is used as a general guide, but its analog companion (i.e., feeling the heat on your skin) is the best way to discover the "right" time[21] of day for various activities. This is because the forecast changes a bit from day to day, and the edges of that right time are somewhat blurry. There are no hard stops and starts—like with an alarm clock—because we are attending to the process of the rising and falling intensity of the sun. We eventually get to a point where the process is over (and now it is undeniably *hot*), but there is some slack in the meantime.

This analog reckoning goes against the broader cultural norm of speed and precision, and instead I have noticed that it invites greater presence. Its holistic approach helps me to keenly focus my attention in order to get things done by the right time—I quite literally "don't have all day." It reflects an agrarian sensibility in this way. Contrary to the view of agrarian work as more relaxed, its tie to temporal rhythms means that what can be done and when it can be done is quite uncompromising. Research led by Gilly Leshed, information science and design scholar , identifies this quality in task accomplishment on a modern organic family farm.[22] She found that participants were adept at weaving together the digital (e.g., time-sensitive school-related events for their children) and the analog (e.g., the times of the day and year when work could be done). Thus, although part of the broader culture that commoditizes time by the clock, they also designed their time on the basis of temporal needs.

We might find places in our own lives where the analog and digital come together, allowing us to transcend culture in the pursuit of a passion. For instance, in my experience as a night owl who often works late into the evening (pushing the edges of what nighttime means), an analog approach to my morning allows me to accomplish several interrelated goals. That is, I am aware of a magical window of time in the summertime when I can wake up fully rested and still get outside for a morning meditation before the temperatures rise too high. It involves a bit of trial and error from month to month, as I test out the edges of the sweltering heat, but it is more useful for my purposes than a purely digital solution (i.e., setting an alarm clock that often interrupts my sleep). It is the best of all worlds. I get to follow my biological clock (i.e., work evenings) and still enjoy the stunning summer sky to begin my day. The whole event and how each part is interrelated (i.e., working late, adequate sleep, hot summers, morning meditation, time outdoors, etc.) drives the design of my day. Possibilities emerge when these are viewed together rather than being focused on any one of these goals as a limitation.

Exclusively digital perspectives similarly draw us away from a holistic understanding of the world and deeper into artificial separations that impede our ability to find designerly solutions. At a cultural level, design wisdom is needed to identify analog solutions that help us manage digitally driven crises of the modern epoch. That innately human drive to find the perfect time in the day or week or year exemplifies one final observation I would like to underscore: Good design takes time and iteration. I elaborate this further in the concluding chapter.

6
Measure Twice: Good Design Takes Time

Measure twice, cut once.

—proverb

The underlying thesis of *Time by Design* (i.e., going slow to go fast) is not a grand social or organizational experiment but rather an enduring principle found across cultures and eras as the surest path to success. For example, in US special operations training, Navy SEALs and Army Rangers are taught "Slow is smooth, smooth is fast." It is the ancient Greek wisdom of Aesop's fable *The Tortoise and the Hare* that teaches "Slow and steady wins the race." It was the counsel of Augustus, the first emperor of ancient Rome, known for admonishing his commanders to *festina lente*, translated as "Make haste, slowly." It was the refrain of America's "winningest" coach, John Wooden, "Be quick, but don't hurry." While writing this book, I repeatedly heard stories of beloved leaders who advised those they led using some version of this fundamental precept. So, despite the easy draw of limited, linear, transactional thinking, those who excel beyond the mundane, who rise above the ordinary to the extraordinary, have always been guided by expanded, nonlinear, transcendent engagement with the world.

Indeed, an age-old proverb with purchase across the field of design, "Measure twice, cut once," extols the speed gained by slowing down to begin any design effort. That is, good design takes time—it starts slow. As I mentioned in chapter 1, the slow communication design logics described in this book are also central to the *work* of design. Neither the ideation process nor the implementation can be rushed. Chronemic design relies upon iteration. Although this is true for design of any kind, when we approach the difficult task of redesigning time, iteration holds new meaning.

When we take iteration seriously, it means becoming comfortable with uncertainty as part of the process.[1] This can be a challenge because time itself is a communication technology that we rely on precisely to increase our sense of certainty and control.[2] Therefore, the very driving force that motivates chronemic design can work against its need for iteration. Nonetheless, the rush to certainty runs contrary to slow communication design logics. Early preoccupation with certainty preempts the power of nonlinearity, transcendence, and inhabiting all time frames. Rather, when we lean into the opportunities that uncertainty permits, we allow for and amplify the design wisdom described in chapter 5. Accordingly, slow CDLs represent a meta-competency for designers as well as for managers and frontline organizational members. In this concluding chapter, I first bring together the various resources developed throughout *Time by Design* in a framework to support those engaged in chronemic design across the iterative spaces of inspiration, ideation, and implementation. Then, I address the ways slow CDL can be used to meet the time-based challenges for the designers, professionals, and organizational members doing this work.

A Comprehensive Multi-Space Framework for Chronemic Design

Speed in collective action is never simply a time-based issue. Throughout *Time by Design*, I have sought to develop its multilayered nature and expose what ultimately drives time-sensitive task accomplishment—that is, its chronemic design. If we simply need a vehicle for information, fast CDLs thrive and deliver speed. This is true for settings such as 911 and the CACTX statewide abuse hotline. However, a range of other tasks that we face rely upon more than information to deliver speed—they rely on relationships. When we need a vehicle fit for relationships, slow CDLs are required. In those cases, speed arrives through expanded time frames, nonlinear trajectories, and the possibility of transcendence. As so much design wisdom conveys—from the earliest tales and aphorisms that span the world—speed is frequently not fast. Indeed, patience is often a prerequisite for speed.

Although conventional organizational theory relies almost exclusively on time-based interventions to speed work along, this reductive approach is effective only over very brief timescales. In contrast, two complementary communication design logics introduced and developed here—that is, fast and slow—illustrate how effective teams, communities, and organizations routinely communicate slow to go fast. In table 6.1, I bring together the tools and insights offered throughout *Time by Design* to help guide chronemic design efforts across the three spaces of innovation Brown describes. This comprehensive multi-space framework includes the detailed, step-by-step toolkit elaborated in chapter 2 and considers it within the larger, iterative chronemic design process—from inspiration to ideation to implementation.

Multiple practicable insights arise from applying this framework across various spaces of design. Initially, from a space of inspiration, identifying *three theories of communication* in a given setting offers us a point of entry to (re)consider our existing communication practices and principles. This theory framework (also contained in the Chronemic Design Toolkit) moves us beyond superficial "more-faster-better" dictates and instead focuses our attention on the ways that our communication norms create our experience of time. This was the awareness that permitted the CAC movement to reenvision and reform how children are protected using a collaborative multidisciplinary

Table 6.1
A comprehensive multi-space framework for chronemic design

Inspiration

i.e., the need to optimize or address chronemic issues arises

3 Theories of Communication	Theory Framework
	• In a given setting, the time frame of interaction unfolds in (a single or multiple) frame(s).
	• In a given setting, the shape of the trajectory between time and interaction is (linear or nonlinear).
	• In a given setting, interaction is (transactional or transcendent).

Ideation

i.e., the process of assessing which chronemic theories best support a setting

3 Features of a Timescape	Features Framework
	• The central *communication process* that a given group or organization needs to support
	• The timescale of the communication process
	• The *time-based dimensions (assumptions and practices)* that support or impede this communication process
3 Specifications of a Task	Task Framework
	• *What?* i.e., the contours of a "task" must become apparent
	• *How?* i.e., an approach or path that enables task accomplishment is determined
	• *Why?* i.e., a purpose focuses the work, acting as a filter regarding what tasks and processes will support or hinder its completion

Implementation

i.e., the experience of putting chronemic designs into practice

3 Realities of Chronemic Design	Design Realities
	• *Inconsistency*—Groups/organizations may be inconsistent in what they describe and what they do
	• *Competition*—Groups/organizations often have competing chronemic designs
	• *Complementarity*—Fast and slow chronemic designs are naturally complementary, each supporting the other

Table 6.1
Continued

3 Signposts to Support Chronemic Design	Implementation Signposts
	• Poorly run organizations give "slow" a bad name
	• Chronemic design must point to a complementary theory of communication
	• A design culture is crucial to leveraging slow communication design logics

team response. This is the discernment that guides the Patient Revolution and their global community of clinicians and patients to create unhurried conversations that transform health care. This was reflected in the strategies described by our lay designers in the everyday digital communication timescape, who implicitly understood the need for both fast and slow CDLs in different settings. It is the rationale behind the Manifesto for Agile Software Development and the reason for its early success. Importantly, the story of Agile also points to the need for continuous attention to the space of implementation in chronemic design, elaborated below.

In the space of ideation, the *three features of a timescape* (elaborated in the Toolkit) prescribe a step-by-step path for chronemic design. For example, applied to the challenges faced in the Safety Net Healthcare timescape, the features framework can be used as a guide to redesign appointments around the communication process (i.e., patient care) rather than trying to fit the communication process into an arbitrary time frame.[3] Through attention to the timescale and the time-based dimensions that diminish patient care, Safety Net Healthcare (and other organizations like it) will better understand the underlying cause of the current challenges they face. As well, through the related toolkit, organizations can redesign time to support key organizational communication processes. For example, in chapter 3, I reflected on how moving from a focus on scarcity to flexibility is one path to improve the delivery of patient care at Safety Net Healthcare.

Additionally, reassessing the *three specifications of a task* offers added leverage in a (re)design effort. Alongside the Chronemic Design Toolkit (that includes the theory framework and features framework), it helps a group or organization gain clarity on an oft-overlooked question: *How?* Although the *what* of a collective is often straightforward (e.g., serving delicious food, manufacturing automobiles, electing a political candidate, etc.), and the *why* is an increasingly common question for organizations to consider (e.g., to satisfy customers, to deliver profits to shareholders, to make the world a better place, etc.), when it comes to *how*, organizations tend to revert to time-based infrastructures[4] (i.e., the way they run the kitchen, their manufacturing processes, the political season, etc.).[5]

As described in chapter 4, relationships are the *how* in settings that rely on slow communication design logics. They are the underlying means of task accomplishment. For instance, key language used throughout the external communication for Safety Net Healthcare indicates that "access to health care" is their *what*. In practice, however, we found that their *how* was exclusively driven by time (i.e., appointment times, waiting times, etc.). On its face, this time-based approach makes sense. However, it creates a self-perpetuating cycle that distracts attention away from the temporality of care. The problem was masquerading as a solution. Although their *why* was laudable—readily and clearly articulated as "equity"—without an accurate understanding of *how*, redesign efforts can easily stall or fail. Therefore, this task framework provides a simple way to identify chronemic design inconsistencies. For instance, if a given setting demands a fast CDL, then a time-based infrastructure would be a proper answer to *how*. However, equitable access to health care points towards a slow CDL that designs time to support relationships through multiple frames of interaction, nonlinear trajectories, and belief in the possibility of transcendence.

In the space of implementation, the *three realities of chronemic design* and the *three signposts to support chronemic design* are useful guidelines to continually revisit after the initial inspiration and ideation spaces. While working with (and within) groups and organizations, these insights are needed to recognize and manage the social and political contours of a setting. The most brilliant chronemic design is only as useful as it is available to members in their day-to-day work. The consistent buy-in and practice needed for successful implementation takes time in various respects. Therefore, in the conclusion below, I offer final reflections to address the ongoing space of implementation.

Conclusion: Good Design Takes Time

Start Slow

As elaborated in chapter 2, design demands iterative processes of reflection and action. Therefore, professional designers will benefit from incorporating slow communication design logics in their work with clients. Indeed, Tim Brown of IDEO advocates that designers reject the efficiencies of convergent thinking and strive for excellence through divergent thinking. He describes, "If the convergent phase of problem solving is what drives us toward solutions, the objective of divergent thinking is to multiply options to create choices. . . . By testing competing ideas against one another, there is an increased likelihood that the outcome will be bolder, more creatively disruptive, and more compelling. Linus Pauling said it best: 'To have a good idea, you must first have lots of ideas'—and he won *two* Nobel Prizes."[6]

Given the prevalence of overwork for many professionals, such as described by scholars Christine Beckman and Melissa Mazmanian in *Dreams of the Overworked*,[7] I want to acknowledge that the call for divergent thinking may appear unsustainable: Ironically, "Who has time for that?" However, Brown doesn't advocate that designers only engage in convergence. He advocates for alternating phases of divergence and convergence in order to work within budgets and timelines. Through this approach, the use of slow CDLs actually facilitates the ability to "get up to speed" in the initial work within oscillating cycles of divergent and convergent thinking. In this way, it yields more time-based efficiencies in the long run. Recall that in chapter 4, I described how MDTs who did not budget for this "slow" time together reported weaker performance and lost communication efficiencies in contrast to those who made the investment. Not only did spending the time *not* increase burnout caused by overwork, it actually helped guard against it.

Practice Presence

An additional ask of slow communication design logics that initially takes time but builds relational resources and efficiencies is *presence*. In *Being Present*, communication scholar Jeanine Turner explains that "social presence describes your feeling of being connected within a specific conversation or interaction."[8] Counterintuitively, focusing on multiple time frames—past, present, and future—simultaneously enhances our present moment awareness.[9] This is because, from a holistic perspective, it contains the raw materials out of which participants build a shared future and honor each other's past. Jocelyn Spence, an interaction design researcher, led a team of researchers and artists who found support for this relationship. Through two case studies, set in the timescape of a museum visit, they asked people to talk about past and future interactions with others. They concluded that "the more a designed experience invited simultaneous mental and emotional investment in the past and future, the more engaged users became in their experience of the 'now.'"[10]

Nelson and Stolterman describe how these qualities of presence emerge through designs via "the emergent essence of the whole." We sense when others are present, and we connect with it. Presence is experiential. It cannot be delineated in an employee manual or a memorandum of understanding, as Mary (a forensic interviewer in the CACTX timescape) explained when asked about the power of

MDT case reviews—that is, you must "come and experience it." However, as we learned from the design of MDTs, we can and we should provide the right set of circumstances to facilitate presence by allotting adequate time for communication. Counter to digital values of transactionalism, linearity, and short-term thinking, presence reflects an analog perspective on human interaction. Ultimately, this is how slow communication design logics become conveyors of soul.

Turner's conceptualization of presence overlaps closely with Eisenberg's description of transcendence detailed in chapter 1. Whereas presence focuses on the experience in the moment as well as the requisite conditions, transcendence extends to the possibilities born of it. Both the quality of presence and the experience of transcendence rely upon mindfulness—a concept elaborated in the next section.

Address Challenges

In addition to starting slow and practicing presence, it is important to design with anticipation of the three challenges to using slow communication design logics (identified in chapter 5):

1. Poorly run organizations give slow communication design logics a bad reputation *so you may encounter resistance to slow.*

2. Underlying theories of communication must complement the design *so a system for ensuring this complementarity must be developed.*

3. A design culture is crucial to success *so this requires long-term commitment.*

1.   Meet the resistance to slow   First, attend to the cultural baggage around going slow to go fast. For instance, despite their success around the globe and nearly thirty years after the children's advocacy centers movement first began, resistance among social services employees who are new to the MDT model is still the norm. The Children's Advocacy Centers of Texas has addressed this resistance through new design innovations to make this challenging work easier for members. Many of these design efforts have set them apart from other children's advocacy centers, and as a result, CACTX has become a national leader in the CAC movement. As an example, through their MDT Enhancement Program, each local CAC was allocated an MDT coordinator to manage and provide leadership for both the information sharing and the collaboration processes upon which MDTs rely. This role helps to smooth the day-to-day logistic and cultural frictions that come with asking people to routinely take an unconventional path to time-sensitive task accomplishment by marrying the linear (i.e., fast response times) and nonlinear (i.e., routine meetings), the short term (i.e., information sharing) and long term (i.e., team building), and the transactional (i.e., 911 or abuse hotline) and transcendent (i.e., joint investigation and collaborative case reviews).

By meeting this resistance with interventions designed to address member agency concerns, CACTX has achieved remarkable growth and success in a relatively short amount of time. In thirty years, they have served more than one million children in the state of Texas alone. They have expanded their capacity to do so by going from $1.5 million in pass-through funding for thirteen CACs with sixty-six staff members who served 7,300 children across forty-four counties in 1994 to nearly $80 million in funding for seventy CACs with 1,554 staff members who served sixty-two thousand children across 208 counties in 2024. Nonetheless, because of the wider culture in which they operate, CACTX and other children's advocacy centers around the globe will continue to encounter resistance to the slow communication design logics that drive their work. This is not a sign of failure. This is a cultural reality that must be openly acknowledged and continually addressed. Rather than shy away from this resistance, CACTX has turned the slow communication design logics upon which their MDTs rely into a core meta-competency for their entire organizational model and for the movement at large. As some evidence, their Statewide Intake Initiative (SWI; i.e., a faster delivery mechanism of reported child abuse cases), MDT Enhancement Program (i.e., the creation of dedicated staff positions to support MDTs and the SWI), and Outcome Measurement System have been adopted by more than nine hundred children's advocacy centers around the United States.

2. Design for complementarity   The successful implementation of chronemic design relies upon fidelity, or complementarity, across the underlying theories of communication found in the various day-to-day policies and practices throughout the organization. In chapters 3 and 5, I gave examples of how some organizations lack this complementarity by design. This might look like an organization trying to convince relevant stakeholders that they center relationships as the means of task accomplishment when, in reality, it is a manipulative ploy designed to create goodwill and compliance. Alternatively, I mentioned in chapter 3 that other well-intentioned organizations who lack resources and infrastructure may find themselves in this situation. Yet another example—and the focus in this section—is a best-case scenario: well-designed and well-run organizations who have achieved the cultural buy-in for successful design implementation and simply need better communication routines in place.

We can think of this as attention to whether the time-based infrastructure includes routines and practices that can be leveraged to ensure this complementarity. For CACTX, this infrastructure is under the direction of the MDT coordinator, who proactively orchestrates an efficient flow of time-sensitive information from the Statewide Intake Initiative as well as an effective collaborative response through the MDT case reviews. Working together with the executive directors who oversee each CAC, this allows for constant alignment (and realignment) of the driving theories of communication at all levels of the organization. The unique needs of every group or organization will demand a different strategy to ensure that their infrastructure includes a means to maintain a high level of chronemic design fidelity. It requires routinely monitoring operations to consider whether both fast and slow communication design logics are being leveraged (in practice) as appropriate and in a complementary fashion.

A familiar example of this need for a stronger time-based infrastructure and related monitoring happens with scheduling medical appointments and whether telemedicine options are offered. This communication setting also illustrates how even a minor design intervention can yield major advantages. As background, research shows that the use of telemedicine appointments can lead to timelier primary care visits,[11] improve clinic show rates,[12] increase access in rural areas,[13] and reduce health disparities.[14] Yet, given the wider availability of telemedicine in recent years, it is one of the most underutilized opportunities to ensure that fast and slow CDLs are being used in a complementary fashion in health care.

When used appropriately, the convenience of telemedicine supports patients' goals both during and after a visit. For patients who rely upon public transportation and/or may hold jobs without adequate time off or sick leave, telemedicine can relieve the burden of routine medical care through less time off of work (or school) and less time in transport. Dr. Urmimala Sarkar (my research collaborator in the Safety Net Healthcare study) shared that some of her patients must take the entire day off of work and travel a great distance just to make it to an in-person appointment. Alternatively, for patients with an energy-limiting chronic illness, telemedicine leaves them with more energy at the end of the day because of the time and energy saved on showering, dressing, and transportation. And patients who live in urban areas overwhelmed by traffic might spend two hours (round trip) in transportation time before they even see a doctor (assuming their appointment is also running on time).

This underutilization of telemedicine when it is medically appropriate runs counter to slow communication design logics, and it can occur due to simple oversight. This happens even in excellent organizations and is an example of day-to-day operational drift away from intended design. Close adherence to both fast and slow CDLs points to the value of telemedicine in several regards. First, attention to multiple time frames means that patients' time before, during, and after the appointment is considered. For example, might the effort involved in attending an in-person appointment make matters worse later (either through the patient coming into contact with a virus while in the waiting room or by triggering a flare-up of a chronic illness)? Or will the patient lose income due to their absence from work? Second, patients may not ask for telemedicine because its availability and usage is still relatively new. Patients are also unlikely to know whether it's medically appropriate for their appointment. Therefore, rather than seeing the process of scheduling appointments as a simple transaction, it is an another (early) opportunity to listen and stay open to possibilities (i.e., transcendence). Finally, a commitment to nonlinearity means that while it might take an extra sixty seconds to screen patients for telemedicine, if it improves appointment timeliness and decreases no-shows, then it ultimately saves time.

I was able to observe how easily this oversight can occur when I scheduled a routine colonoscopy after turning fifty. In the midst of a busy week, I received a referral call from the gastroenterology practice. Wanting to have the procedure done before the new semester got underway, I quickly shared my availability and which of the two locations offered was closest to me. The scheduler then told me that the first appointment was just a consultation with the doctor and that I would have to wait until the appointment to schedule the procedure. Surprised at this delay, I acquiesced and agreed to the earliest available appointment, even though it was the location farthest from my house. Reluctantly, I drove more than half an hour to the appointment to meet the gastroenterologist of whom my general practitioner spoke so highly. I stayed curious and open, wondering why a consultation was needed for such a routine procedure.

After the five-minute appointment in which the physician simply overviewed the procedure in a way I could have read online from the comfort of my home, my curiosity was piqued. She asked if I had any questions, and I did. After some pleasantries, I asked her if there was a reason that her office doesn't take advantage of telemedicine for routine appointments such as mine. A knowing look came over her face, and she said that I should have been offered a telemedicine option. She then went on to say that in the last year, they had also made an option available on their website for patients to bypass any consultation appointment altogether and schedule the colonoscopy directly. She shared that sometimes people are anxious about the procedure for a number of reasons and (when slow CDLs matter) want to meet face-to-face with their doctor, but that to speed up the larger scheduling process, they were proud of having made the transition to online scheduling as a (fast CDL) option. Nonetheless, despite the best efforts of the doctors in her practice, the organization lacked complementarity between their intended chronemic design (i.e., catering to patients' unique needs through both fast and slow CDLs) and the day-to-day practices of frontline organizational members (i.e., routine scheduling practices for all patients that privileges speed rather than specificity).

This lack of fidelity across different functional units in an organization is a common issue, not based on malicious intent but rather due to a lack of attention or mindfulness. Management scholars Karl Weick and Kathleen Sutcliffe brought attention to this challenge through their research on high-reliability organizations and the mindful organizing that sustains them. Although Weick and Sutcliffe's work was developed in the context of organizations that face extreme environments, such as nuclear aircraft carriers and wildland firefighting, they propose that all organizations can benefit from the same five principles: preoccupation with failure, reluctance to simplify, sensitivity to operations, commitment to resilience, and deference to expertise. I draw attention to mindful organizing because

Weick and Sutcliffe point to the centrality of "relationships and con-tinuous conversation" in achieving the first three of these aims and they illustrate how speed is often achieved through investing needed time in key organizational communication processes. They explain that mindful organizations "are sensitive to and constantly adjust to small cues or mishaps that if left unaddressed, could accumulate and interact with other parts of the system resulting in larger problems."[15]

The chronemic design lesson inherent in Weick and Sutcliffe's research on mindful organizing is that it takes time to avoid compla-cency and the rush to certainty. Without regular, routine attention to the underlying theories of communication in an organization that are being tolerated and rewarded, the lure of fast theories will prevail. This was predicted by Weber's iron cage described in chapter 1 and Ritzer's McDonaldization and Amazonization described in chapter 3. In order to nurture and maintain theories of communication that support the intended design, organizational members must be alert to inconsistencies in what their organizations say they do and what they actually do.

3. Cultivate a design culture   Each of the previous two challenges—reducing resistance to slow and designing for complementarity—is mutually interdependent, with a third challenge that must be addressed to successfully implement chronemic design: cultivate a design culture. This is also an iterative process that takes time (and persistence). Notably, it relies upon design wisdom and embraces uncertainty.

I observed an excellent example of how this design wisdom exists as both an individual and collective accomplishment as one of my research collaborators in the Safety Net Healthcare case study, Dr. Michelle-Linh Nguyen, sat out to open her own independent medical practice. Her work is driven by the broader vision of host-ing a virtual community of doctors (located around the country and world) who collectively practice and share what Nguyen refers to as the wisdom, craft, and soul needed to reimagine and redesign industrial health care. The various resources that she curates are generated through ongoing conversations with the members of this community, including advice for new doctors and other reflections on the practice of medicine (from the perspective of both patients and doctors). Aware of its iterative and ongoing nature, she routinely releases new and expanded versions of these resources. Additionally, as she documents the many months leading up to the launch of her own medical practice, she features and normalizes uncertainty as an unavoidable part of redesigning health-care delivery.

Nguyen is building her organization around a design culture from its very conception. Other organizational members and leaders will be asked to build a design culture within existing institutions that actively resist analog (i.e., differentiated, holistic, complex) solutions because of the iron cage that Max Weber[16] foresaw a century ago. Large organizations tend toward digital solutions because they are efficient (if not effective) and fit easily into existing structures: These solutions may not be great, but they will get the job done and won't hold up the line. Therefore, unlike the community of "like-valued" people that Nguyen has brought together, in other instances, cultivating a design culture will demand bringing people along who initially resist.

Meeting these challenges in fostering a design culture and the patience that it requires is exemplified in a story I heard while visiting the local Austin-based children's advocacy center called the Center for Child Protection—that is, one of the seventy member centers of CACTX. At the close of our facility tour, we got to enjoy some time with Mickler, a yellow labrador/golden retriever mix who works as an emotional support animal for the children they serve. Although the need for Mickler (and dogs like him) might seem obvious to many, it was not obvious to the court system or various state agencies when the idea was first presented. The woman who led the tour said that when they initially asked for permission to use an emotional support animal, they encountered the same answer: "No, no, no. You can't do that. You can't do that." To this refrain, the center leadership continually replied, "Let's try. Let's try." And eventually, step by step, office by office, it worked. She described this as part of a larger ethos that drives their work at their CAC. When they encounter resistance to their mission (i.e., serving children to the greatest of their ability), they offer, "Let's try."

Summary

Even as the dominant ethos is a fast communication design logic—characterized by more-faster-better and the continual acceleration of work through ever-greater technologically driven efficiencies—the very speed we crave is rooted in the often-overlooked foundations of slow communication design logics. Echoed in design wisdom across cultures and centuries, the best and brightest have always harnessed the power of going slow to go fast. Indeed, throughout *Time by Design*, I highlight the inherent complementarity of fast and slow CDL.

To make these two logics more accessible to designers, organizational members, and practitioners, the Chronemic Design Toolkit introduced here offers a step-by-step approach to build time around the communication process it is intended to support. Additionally, a Comprehensive Framework for Chronemic Design guides users in the overlapping, iterative spaces of inspiration, ideation, and implementation. From recognizing the need to optimize a chronemic issue in a group or organization, to assessing which chronemic theories best support a setting, to navigating the realities of putting chronemic designs into practice, this framework and the chapters from which it draws offer guidance at multiple points in the design process.

Beyond the logistic and strategic support these tools provide, each serves to remind us of a greater insight: Time is a design of our own making. As such, we can (and should) remake it to better support our lives, organizations, and communities. The way forward is not a binary choice between either fast or slow communication design logics but rather a harmonious integration of both, recognizing their mutual interdependence.

Notes

Chapter 1

1. Edward T. Hall, *The Silent Language* (Anchor Books, 1959).

2. Thomas Bruneau, "Chronemics," in *Encyclopedia of Communication Theory*, ed. S. W. Littlejohn and K. A. Foss (Sage, 2009), 96–101.

3. J. Christopher Jones, "Thoughts About the Context of Designing," *Design Studies* 1, no. 3 (1980): 5.

4. Nobel Assembly at Karolinska Institutet, "The 2017 Nobel Prize in Physiology or Medicine," October 2, 2017, http://www.nobelprize.org/nobel_prizes/medicine /laureates/2017/press.html.

5. Eviatar Zerubavel, *The Seven Day Circle: The History and Meaning of the Week* (University of Chicago Press, 1989).

6. Émile Durkheim, *The Elementary Forms of the Religious Life*, trans. Joseph Ward Swain (Free Press, 1968), 23.

7. Big Medium, "Betelhem Makonnen, *Rock Standard Time (RST)*," 2020, https:// www.bigmedium.org/rock-standard-time; and Glasstire, "Five-Minute Tours: Betelhem Makonnen at Big Medium, Austin, August 27, 2020, https://glasstire.com/2020 /08/27/five-minute-tours-betelhem-makonnen-at-big-medium-austin/.

8. Allen C. Bluedorn, *The Human Organization of Time: Temporal Realities and Experience* (Stanford Business Books, 2002).

9. Nobel Assembly at Karolinska Institutet, "The 2017 Nobel Prize in Physiology or Medicine."

10. Manuel Castells, *The Rise of the Network Society*, 2nd ed. (Blackwell, 2000).

11. Thomas Hylland Eriksen, *Tyranny of the Moment Fast and Slow Time in the Information Age* (Pluto Press, 2001).

12. Max Weber, *The Protestant Ethic and the Spirit of Capitalism*, trans. Talcott Parsons (Roxbury, 1996).

13. Christopher M. Barnes, Kaifeng Jiang, and David P. Lepak, "Sabotaging the Benefits of Our Own Human Capital: Work Unit Characteristics and Sleep," *Journal of Applied Psychology* 101, no. 2 (2016): 209–221.

14. Sarah Norgate, *Beyond 9 to 5: Your Life in Time*, Maps of the Mind (Weidenfeld & Nicolson, 2006).

15. Chris Yuill and Natascha Mueller-Hirth, "Paperwork, Compassion and Temporal Conflicts in British Social Work," *Time & Society* 28, no. 4 (2019): 1532–1551.

16. Michelle A. Barton and William A. Kahn, "Group Resilience: The Place and Meaning of Relational Pauses," *Organization Studies* 40, no. 9 (2019): 1409–1429; Alex Soojung-Kim Pang, *Rest: Why You Get More Done When You Work Less* (Basic Books, 2016); and Yousra Rahmouni Elidrissi and David Courpasson, "Body Breakdowns as Politics: Identity Regulation in a High-Commitment Activist Organization," *Organization Studies* 42, no. 1 (2021): 35–59, https://doi.org/10.1177/0170840619867729.

17. Mark Aakhus, "Communication as Design," *Communication Monographs* 74, no. 1 (2007): 112–117, https://doi.org/10.1080/03637750701196383.

18. S. E. Little, "The Role of Time Frames in Design Decision-Making," *Design Studies* 8, no. 3 (1987): 170–182, https://doi.org/10.1016/0142-694X(87)90039-1.

19. Mark Aakhus and Sally Jackson, "Technology, Interaction, and Design," in *Handbook of Language and Social Interaction*, ed. Kristine L. Fitch and Robert E. Sanders (Lawrence Erlbaum Associates), 411–436.

20. Aakhus, "Communication as Design," 112.

21. For a detailed discussion of recursivity, see Anthony Giddens, *The Constitution of Society: Outline of the Theory of Structuration* (University of California Press, 1984), 2.

22. Durkheim, *The Elementary Forms of the Religious Life*, 23.

23. Pierre Bourdieu, *Outline of a Theory of Practice* (Cambridge University Press, 1972).

24. In chapter 2, "Design Frames," I describe how Dr. Victor Montori, author of *Why We Revolt*, aims to challenge this premise and redesign medical care to take temporal processes into account; Victor Montori, *Why We Revolt: A Patient Revolution for Careful*

and Kind Care, 2nd ed. (Mayo Clinic Press, 2020). Personally, I never trust a physician who always runs on time.

25. Kerk F. Kee, Bethanie Le, and Kulsawasd Jitkajornwanich, "If You Build It, Promote It, and They Trust You, Then They Will Come: Diffusion Strategies for Science Gateways and Cyberinfrastructure Adoption to Harness Big Data in the Science, Technology, Engineering, and Mathematics (STEM) Community," *Concurrency and Computation: Practice and Experience* 33, no. 19 (2021): e6192, https://doi.org/10.1002/cpe.6192; and Kerk F. Kee and Andrew R. Schrock, "Best Social and Organizational Practices of Successful Science Gateways and Cyberinfrastructure Projects," *Future Generation Computer Systems* 94 (2019): 795–801, https://doi.org/10.1016/j.future.2018.04.063.

26. Kee and Schrock, "Best Social and Organizational Practices," 798.

27. Kee et al., "If You Build It, Promote It," 18.

28. Kee et al., "If You Build It, Promote It," 15.

29. Aakhus and Jackson, "Technology, Interaction, and Design," 413.

30. Carolyn F. Strauss and Alastair Fuad-Luke, "The Slow Design Principles: A New Interrogative and Reflexive Tool for Design Research and Practice," paper presented at *Changing the Change: Design Visions, Proposals and Tools*, Turin, Italy, 2008.

31. Carl Honoré, *In Praise of Slowness: How a Worldwide Movement Is Challenging the Cult of Speed* (Harper Collins, 2004).

32. Dawna I. Ballard and Ana Aguilar, "When Pacing Is a Privilege: The Time Scale of Exclusion," in *Organizing Inclusion: Moving Diversity from Demographics to Communication Processes*, ed. Marya L. Doerfel, and Jennifer L. Gibbs (Routledge), 90–112; Barton and Kahn, "Group Resilience"; Lillian Su, Seth Kaplan, Randall Burd, Carolyn Winslow, Amber Hargrove, and Mary Waller, "Trauma Resuscitation: Can Team Behaviours in the Prearrival Period Predict Resuscitation Performance?," *BMJ Simulation & Technology Enhanced Learning* 3, no. 3 (2017): 106–110, https://doi.org/10.1136/bmjstel-2016-000143; and Sjir Uitdewilligen and Mary J. Waller, "Information Sharing and Decision-Making in Multidisciplinary Crisis Management Teams," *Journal of Organizational Behavior* 39, no. 6 (2018): 731–748, https://doi.org/10.1002/job.2301.

33. Karl E. Weick, "A Bias for Conversation: Acting Discursively in Organizations," in *The SAGE Handbook of Organizational Discourse*, ed. C. Oswick et al. (Sage, 2004), 405–412.

34. James D. Thompson, *Organizations in Action* (McGraw-Hill, 1967).

35. Susan Lund, James Manyika, and Sree Ramaswamy, "Preparing for a New Era of Knowledge Work," *McKinsey Quarterly* 4, no. 1 (2012): 103–110.

36. Dawna I. Ballard and Thomas McVey, "Measure Twice, Cut Once: The Temporality of Communication Design," *Journal of Applied Communication Research* 42, no. 2 (2014): 190–207, https://doi.org/10.1080/00909882.2013.874571.

37. Su et al., "Trauma Resuscitation," 108.

38. Su et al., "Trauma Resuscitation," 2.

39. Su et al., "Trauma Resuscitation," 2.

40. Dron Manojkumar Mandhana, "Multi-factor Model of the Antecedents of Unplanned Conversations at Work," *International Journal of Organization Theory & Behavior* 27, no. 3 (2024): 263–280.

41. Steve Whittaker, David Frohlich, and Owen Daly-Jones, "Informal Workplace Communication: What Is It Like and How Might We Support It?," in *Conference Companion on Human Factors in Computing Systems*, ed. Catherine Plaisant (Association for Computing Machinery, 1994), 131–137.

42. Cliff Oswick and David Richards, "Talk in Organizations: Local Conversations, Wider Perspectives," *Culture and Organization* 10, no. 2 (2004): 107–123, https://doi.org/10.1080/14759550420002533404.

43. Mandhana, "Multi-factor Model of the Antecedents of Unplanned Conversations at Work," 13.

44. Eric M. Eisenberg, "Jamming: Transcendence Through Organizing," *Communication Research* 17, no. 2 (1990): 139, https://doi.org/10.1177/009365090017002001.

45. Mihaly Csikszentmihalyi, *Finding Flow: The Psychology of Engagement with Everyday Life* (Hachette UK, 2020).

46. Eisenberg, "Jamming," 147.

47. Andrew W. Ishak and Dawna I. Ballard, "Time to Re-Group: A Typology and Nested Phase Model for Action Teams," *Small Group Research* 43, no. 1 (2012): 3–29, https://doi.org/10.1177/1046496411425250.

48. Dawna I. Ballard and David R. Seibold, "Organizational Members' Communication and Temporal Experience: Scale Development and Validation," *Communication Research* 31, no. 2 (2004): 135–172, https://doi.org/10.1177/0093650203261504.

Chapter 2

1. Kees Dorst, *Frame Innovation: Create New Thinking by Design* (MIT Press, 2015).

2. IMDb, "Marin Scorsese Quotes," https://www.imdb.com/name/nm0000217/quotes/.

3. Ida H. J. Sabelis, "Time Sensitivity: A Delicate and Crucial Starting Point of Reflexive Methods for Studying Time in Management and Organization," in *Time in Organizational Research*, ed. Robert Roe, Mary J. Waller, and Stewart Clegg (Routledge, 2009), 167–185.

4. Sabelis, "Time Sensitivity," 177.

5. Srilata Zaheer, Stuart Albert, and Akbar Zaheer, "Time Scales and Organizational Theory," *The Academy of Management Review* 24, no. 4 (1999): 725, https://doi.org /10.5465/AMR.1999.2553250.

6. Jörgen Rahm-Skågeby and Lina Rahm, "HCI and Deep Time: Toward Deep Time Design Thinking," *Human–Computer Interaction* 37, no. 1 (2022): 15–28.

7. The Anthropocene Working Group was formed because there was disagreement between geologists and environmentalists over whether the current epoch we inhabit is the Holocene or the Anthropocene—a term introduced in 2000 by Eugene Stoermer and Paul Crutzen, a Nobel laureate.

8. Alexandra Witze, "Geologists Reject the Anthropocene as Earth's New Epoch— After 15 Years of Debate," *Nature* 627, no. 8003 (2024): 249–250.

9. This is where Ida Sabelis first presented her work on the importance of focus and zoom in developing temporal sensitivity.

10. Note that this subjective judgment still used an objective time scale—i.e., we looked at the number of hours we had been dining and the time on the clock, 11:00 p.m., to guide our decision. Social phenomena often involve subjective judgments based on clock-time norms and its objective hours.

11. Ballard and Seibold, "Organizational Members' Communication and Temporal Experience."

12. Sendhil Mullainathan and Eldar Shafir, *Scarcity: Why Having Too Little Means So Much* (Macmillan, 2013).

13. Ray H. Rosenman and Meyer Friedman, "Modifying Type A Behavior Pattern," *Journal of Psychosomatic Research* 21, no. 4 (1977): 323–331, https://doi.org/10.1016 /0022-3999(77)90015-0.

14. Yoram M. Kalman, Dawna I. Ballard, and Ana M. Aguilar, "Chronemic Urgency in Everyday Digital Communication," *Time & Society* 30, no. 2 (2021), https://doi .org/10.1177/0961463X20987721.

15. Brian Stelter (Reliable Sources), "'Social Dilemma' Star: Social Media is Getting Aggressive as Attention Runs Out," *CNN* video, 1:55, February 25, 2022, https:// www.cnn.com/videos/media/2022/02/13/tristan-harris-social-dilemma-facebook -snapchat-instagram-tiktok-attention-rs-vpx.cnn.

16. Bluedorn, *The Human Organization of Time*, 114.

17. Allen C. Bluedorn and Stephen P. Ferris, "Temporal Depth, Age, and Organizational Performance," in *Fighting for Time: Shifting Boundaries of Work and Social Life*, ed. Cynthia Fuchs Epstein and Arne L. Kalleberg (Russell Sage Foundation, 2004), 149.

18. Bluedorn and Ferris, "Temporal Depth," 116.

19. Adrian Daub, "The Disruption Con: Why Big Tech's Favourite Buzzword is Nonsense," *Guardian* (UK edition), September 24, 2020, https://www.theguardian .com/news/2020/sep/24/disruption-big-tech-buzzword-silicon-valley-power; Nitasha Tiku, "An Alternative History of Silicon Valley Disruption," *Wired*, October 22, 2018, https://www.wired.com/story/alternative-history-of-silicon-valley-disruption /; Laura Sydell, "Tech Industry Confronts a Backlash Against 'Disruptive Innovation,'" *NPR*, January 28, 2019, https://www.npr.org/sections/thetwo-way/2019/01 /28/689198803/tech-industry-confronts-a-backlash-against-disruptive-innovation; and Jill Lepore, "The Disruption Machine," *New Yorker*, June 16, 2014, https://www .newyorker.com/magazine/2014/06/23/the-disruption-machine.

20. James G. March, "Exploration and Exploitation in Organizational Learning," *Organization Science* 2, no. 1 (1991): 71–87, https://doi.org/10.1287/orsc.2.1.71.

21. Ludvig Levasseur, Abbie J. Shipp, Yitzhak Fried, Denise M. Rousseau, and Philip G. Zimbardo, "New Perspectives on Time Perspective and Temporal Focus," *Journal of Organizational Behavior* 41, no. 3 (2020): 235–243, https://doi.org/10.1002 /job.2435.

22. Keith Ferrazzi, "Evaluating the Employees You Can't See," *Harvard Business Review*, December 20, 2012, https://hbr. org/2012/12/evaluating-the-employees-you-c.

23. Richard Feloni, "A Zappos Employee Had the Company's Longest Customer-Service Call at 10 Hours, 43 Minutes," *Business Insider*, July 26, 2016, https://www .businessinsider.com/zappos-employee-sets-record-for-longest-customer-service-call -2016-7.

24. Eyal Ophir, Clifford Nass, and Anthony D. Wagner, "Cognitive Control in Media Multitaskers," in *Proceedings of the National Academy of Sciences of the United States of America* 106, no. 37 (2009): 15583–15587.

25. Gloria Mark, "Multitasking in the Digital Age," *Synthesis Lectures on Human-Centered Informatics* 8, no. 3 (2015): 1–113.

26. Dawna I. Ballard, Dina I. Ramgolam, and Estee Solomon Gray, "Modern Times, Modern Spaces: Interaction Genres and Multiminding in Network-Based Work," in *Work Pressures: New Agendas in Communication*, ed. Dawna I. Ballard and Matthew S. McGlone (Routledge, 2017), 91–108.

27. Ioana C. Cristea and Paul M. Leonardi, "Get Noticed and Die Trying: Signals, Sacrifice, and the Production of Face Time in Distributed Work," *Organization Science* 30, no. 3 (2019): 552–572, https://doi.org/10.1287/orsc.2018.1265.

28. Eviatar Zerubavel, *Hidden Rhythms: Schedules and Calendars in Social Life* (University of Chicago Press, 1981).

29. Alex Pasternack, "How the Master Clock Sets Time for the World," *Vice*, November 6, 2014, https://www.vice.com/en/article/3dkd5b/demetrios-matsakis-and-the -master-clock.

30. Ballard and Seibold, "Organizational Members' Communication and Temporal Experience."

31. Larissa Pschetz and Michelle Bastian, "Temporal Design: Rethinking Time in Design," *Design Studies* 56 (2018): 169–184, https://doi.org/10.1016/j.destud.2017 .10.007.

32. Barbara Adam, *Timewatch: The Social Analysis of Time* (John Wiley, 2013).

33. Aakhus, "Communication as Design."

34. Montori, *Why We Revolt*.

35. Montori, *Why We Revolt*, 131.

36. Dawna I. Ballard, Dron M. Mandhana, Yohanna Tesfai, et al., "Unhurried Conversations in Healthcare Are More Important Than Ever: Identifying Key Communication Practices for Careful and Kind Care," *The Annals of Family Medicine* 22, no. 6 (2024): 533–538.

37. Montori, *Why We Revolt*, 15–16 (italics in the original).

38. Montori, *Why We Revolt*, 130.

39. Aakhus, "Communication as Design," 114.

40. Emma M. Templeton, Luke J. Chang, Elizabeth A. Reynolds, Marie D. Cone LeBeaumont, and Thalia Wheatley, "Fast Response Times Signal Social Connection in Conversation," in *Proceedings of the National Academy of Sciences of the United States of America* 119, no. 4 (2022): e2116915119, https://doi.org/10.1073/pnas.2116915119.

41. Montori, *Why We Revolt*, 92.

42. Montori, *Why We Revolt*, 131.

43. Montori, *Why We Revolt*, 133.

44. Montori, *Why We Revolt*, 131.

45. Montori, *Why We Revolt*, 134.

46. Montori, *Why We Revolt*, 133.

47. Montori, *Why We Revolt*, 133.

48. Montori, *Why We Revolt*, 133.

49. Montori, *Why We Revolt*, 132.

50. Montori, *Why We Revolt*, 133.

51. Montori, *Why We Revolt*, 134.

52. Harold G. Nelson and Erik Stolterman, *The Design Way: Intentional Change in an Unpredictable World* (MIT Press, 2014).

53. Nelson and Stolterman, *The Design Way*, 120.

54. Nelson and Stolterman, *The Design Way*, 121–122.

55. Tim Brown, *Change by Design: How Design Thinking Transforms Organizations and Inspires Innovation*, revised and updated (Harper Collins, 2019), 22.

Chapter 3

1. Henry Blodget, "Mark Zuckerberg on Innovation," *Business Insider*, October 1, 2009, https://www.businessinsider.com/mark-zuckerberg-innovation-2009-10.

2. Nelson and Stolterman, *The Design Way*.

3. Mullainathan and Shafir, *Scarcity*.

4. Aakhus, "Communication as Design."

5. Kim Parker and Juliana Menasce Horowitz, "Majority of Workers Who Quit a Job in 2021 Cite Low Pay, No Opportunities for Advancement, Feeling Disrespected," *Pew Research Center* (blog), March 23, 2022, https://www.pewresearch.org/fact-tank/2022/03/09/majority-of-workers-who-quit-a-job-in-2021-cite-low-pay-no-opportunities-for-advancement-feeling-disrespected/.

6. Frederick Winslow Taylor, *Scientific Management* (Harper & Row, 1911).

7. Max Weber traced the design of industrial organizations to monarchies and military organizations. So, these approaches were not new but were adapted for a new purpose.

8. Note that all twelve dimensions of time exist in every timescape because they exist on a continuum, as described in chapter 2. For instance, the dimension of speed can be characterized as fast, slow, or moderate. Similarly, if flexibility is not a prominent quality in a timescape, then rigidity will be, and so on. However, because the dimensions work like lenses that focus time in particular ways, there may be one

or a few dimensions that are especially powerful in the chronemic design. Accordingly, I will highlight one or two dimensions most central in telling organizational actors how to behave or what to assume.

9. Peter G. Dominick, Dimitra Iordanoglou, Gregory Prastacos, and Richard R. Reilly, "Espoused Values of the 'Fortune 100 Best Companies to Work For': Essential Themes and Implementation Practices," *Journal of Business Ethics* 173, no. 1 (2021): 69–88.

10. Urmimala Sakar, M.D., Elizabeth Jacobs, M.D., Michael Pignone, M.D., Michelle-Linh Nguyen, M.D., Ana Aguilar, M.A., Kate Sebastian, R.N., M.P.H., Anastazja Harris, M.A. and Deepak Maharaj, D.O.

11. It is a Federally Qualified Health Center (FQHC).

12. Richard L. Kravitz, "From the Editors' Desk: Medicine as a Service Industry," *Journal of General Internal Medicine* 25, no. 4 (2010): 279, https://doi.org/10.1007/s11606-010-1282-4.

13. Medicare is a government national health insurance program in the United States.

14. Paul J. DiMaggio and Walter W. Powell, "The Iron Cage Revisited: Institutional Isomorphism and Collective Rationality in Organizational Fields," *American Sociological Review* 48, no. 2 (1983): 147–160.

15. There was one exception. One physician told us that twenty minutes was more than enough time to carry out their work effectively.

16. Taking their suggestions into account, I offer a reprise at the end of this section about how the lens of flexibility could be used to redesign their work.

17. Although patients are scheduled for twenty-minute appointments, only a fraction of that time is spent in provider–patient communication.

18. Ronald E. Rice and Stephen D. Cooper, *Organizations and Unusual Routines: A Systems Analysis of Dysfunctional Feedback Processes* (Cambridge University Press, 2010).

19. Dawna I. Ballard and David R. Seibold, "The Experience of Time at Work: Relationship to Communication Load, Job Satisfaction, and Interdepartmental Communication," *Communication Studies* 57, no. 3 (2006): 317–340.

20. Mullainathan and Shafir, *Scarcity*.

21. Mullainathan and Shafir, *Scarcity*, 7.

22. JAMA Career Center and AMA Moving Medicine, "Physicians and the Great Resignation—A Great Reprioritization," March 2022, https://careers.jamanetwork.com/article/physicians-and-the-great-resignation-a-great-reprioritization-ama-moving-medicine-podcast-.

23. Tiffany O'Callaghan, "Night Special: Why They Call It the Graveyard Shift," *New Scientist (1971)* 220, no. 2945 (2013): 40–41, https://doi.org/10.1016/S0262–4079 (13)62800–6.

24. Miriah Steiger, Timir J. Bharucha, Sukrit Venkatagiri, Martin J. Riedl, and Matthew Lease, "The Psychological Well-Being of Content Moderators: The Emotional Labor of Commercial Moderation and Avenues for Improving Support," paper presented at the *CHI Conference on Human Factors in Computing Systems*, Yokohama, Japan, May 8–13, 2021, https://doi.org/10.1145/3411764.3445092.

25. Mary C. Vance and Joel D. Howell, "Shell Shock and PTSD: A Tale of Two Diagnoses," *Mayo Clinic Proceedings* 95, no. 9 (2020): 1827–1830, https://doi.org/10.1016 /j.mayocp.2020.06.002.

26. Informant interviews refer to participants who are insiders in a given setting. They are "experienced and savvy in the scene, can articulate stories and explanations that others would not, and are especially friendly and open to providing information"; Sarah J. Tracy, *Qualitative Research Methods: Collecting Evidence, Crafting Analysis, Communicating Impact* (Wiley-Blackwell, 2019), 140.

27. Ben McGrath, "Does Football Have a Future? The NFL and the Concussion Crisis," *New Yorker*, January 31, 2011, https://www.newyorker.com/magazine/2011 /01/31/does-football-have-a-future.

28. Dina Inman Ramgolam, PhD, and Sunshine Webster, PhD, helped to supervise and coordinate eight undergraduates (Dave Bryant, Kristin Green, Pauline Mar, Nathaniel (Tre) Newton, and Sarah Sparks). Graduate students, including Jason Flowers, Ashley Barrett, Sarah Rogers, Carley Whitson, and Leah Brisco, also conducted initial interviews and helped me to pilot and revise the interview protocol.

29. Robert W. Turner II, *Not For Long: The Life and Career of the NFL Athlete* (Oxford University Press, 2018), 71.

30. Kim T. Mueser, Paul R. Yarnold, and Fred B. Bryant, "Type A Behaviour and Time Urgency: Perception of Time Adjectives," *British Journal of Medical Psychology* 60, no. 3 (1987): 267–269.

31. Teresa Ghilarducci, "How Many Years Do You Have to Work Before You Retire?," *Forbes*, May 28, 2021, https://www.forbes.com/sites/teresaghilarducci/2021 /05/28/how-many-years-do-you-have-to-work-before-you-retire/?sh=6f5aee60706d.

32. Reem Abdalazem, "This Is the Lowest Paid Player in the NFL: Is There a Minimum Salary in American Football?," February 9, 2025, https://en.as.com/nfl/who-is -the-lowest-paid-player-in-the-nfl-is-there-a-minimum-salary-in-american-football -n/. For example, the median salary in 2021 was $860K. This has gone up dramatically in recent years due to the collective bargaining agreement that went into effect in 2011.

33. NFL Concussion Settlement, "Welcome to the Official NFL Concussion Settlement Website," https://www.nflconcussionsettlement.com. Accessed April 14, 2025.

34. Kurt Streeter, "We're All Complicit in the N.F.L.'s Violent Spectacle," *New York Times*, January 3, 2023, https://www.nytimes.com/2023/01/03/sports/football/nfl-broadcast-fans.html.

35. Elidrissi and Courpasson, "Body Breakdowns as Politics."

36. Karl E. Weick and Kathleen M. Sutcliffe, *Managing the Unexpected: Sustained Performance in a Complex World*, 3rd ed. (John Wiley, 2015).

37. John Hartley, "The Frequencies of Public Writing: Tomb, Tome, and Time as Technologies of the Public," in *Democracy and New Media*, ed. Henry Jenkins and David Thorburn (MIT Press, 2003).

38. Yoram M. Kalman, Gilad Ravid, Daphne R. Raban, and Sheizaf Rafaeli, "Pauses and Response Latencies: A Chronemic Analysis of Asynchronous CMC," *Journal of Computer-Mediated Communication* 12, no. 1 (2006): 1–23, https://doi.org/10.1111/j.1083-6101.2006.00312.x.

39. This included Google Answers (answers to questions posted in an online commercial forum), email sent by employees at Enron (made publicly available) across four years, and discussions among university students enrolled in the same course.

40. Yoram M. Kalman and Sheizaf Rafaeli, "Online Pauses and Silence: Chronemic Expectancy Violations in Written Computer-Mediated Communication," *Communication Research* 38, no. 1 (2010): 54–69, https://doi.org/10.1177/0093650210378229.

41. Bruneau, "Chronemics."

42. Cal Newport, *Deep Work: Rules for Focused Success in a Distracted World* (Hachette UK, 2016).

43. Brian X. Chen, "In Busy Silicon Valley, Protein Powder Is in Demand," *New York Times*, May 25, 2015, https://www.nytimes.com/2015/05/25/technology/in-busy-silicon-valley-protein-powder-is-in-demand.html.

44. Zerubavel, *Hidden Rhythms*.

45. George Ritzer, *The McDonaldization of Society: Into the Digital Age* (Sage, 2021), 2.

Chapter 4

1. Edward T. Hall, *The Dance of Life: The Other Dimension of Time* (Anchor Books, 1983).

2. Hall, *The Dance of Life*, 46–47.

3. Hall, *The Dance of Life*, 49.

4. Allen C. Bluedorn, "An Interview with Anthropologist Edward T. Hall," *Journal of Management Inquiry* 7, no. 2 (1998): 109–115.

5. Agile Manifesto, "Manifesto for Agile Software Development," last modified in 2001, https://agilemanifesto.org.

6. Items on the left were enlarged to emphasize their primacy and value over the more conventionally valued norms on the right.

7. Agile Manifesto, "Principles."

8. Agile Manifesto, "History."

9. Timothy R. Clark, "Agile Doesn't Work Without Psychological Safety," *Harvard Business Review*, February 21, 2022, https://hbr.org/2022/02/agile-doesnt-work-without-psychological-safety; and Peggy Gregory Leonor Barroca, Katie Taylor, Dina Salah, and Helen Sharp, "Agile Challenges in Practice: A Thematic Analysis," in *Agile Processes in Software Engineering and Extreme Programming: 16th International Conference, XP 2015, Helsinki, Finland, May 25–29, 2015, Proceedings 16* (Springer, 2015), 64–80.

10. PragDave, "Agile Is Dead (Long Live Agility)," March 4, 2014, https://pragdave.me/thoughts/active/2014-03-04-time-to-kill-agile.html#fn2.

11. Simple Thread, "Agile at 20: The Failed Rebellion," July 23, 2021, https://www.simplethread.com/agile-at-20-the-failed-rebellion/.

12. Ron Jeffries, "Developers Should Abandon Agile," May 10, 2018, https://ronjeffries.com/articles/018-01ff/abandon-1/.

13. JoAnna Elmquist, Ryan C. Shorey, Jeniimarie Febresm et al., "A Review of Children's Advocacy Centers' (CACs) Response to Cases of Child Maltreatment in the United States," *Aggression and Violent Behavior* 25 (2015): 26–34, https://doi.org/10.1016/j.avb.2015.07.002; and Daniel W. Smith, Tricia H. Witte, and Adrienne E. Fricker-Elhai, "Service Outcomes in Physical and Sexual Abuse Cases: A Comparison of Child Advocacy Center-Based and Standard Services," *Child Maltreatment* 11, no. 4 (2006): 354–360, https://doi.org/10.1177/1077559506292277.

14. Lisa B. Johnson, "A Qualitative Study of Communication Among Child Advocacy Multidisciplinary Team Members Using a Web-Based Case Tracking System," *Journal of Technology in Human Services* 31, no. 4 (2013): 355–367, https://doi.org/10.1080/15228835.2013.861783.

15. Lisa M. Jones, Theodore P. Cross, Wendy A. Walsh, and Monique Simone, "Do Children's Advocacy Centers Improve Families' Experiences of Child Sexual Abuse Investigations?" *Child Abuse & Neglect* 31, no. 10 (2007): 1069–1085, https://doi.org/10.1016/j.chiabu.2007.07.003; and Poonam Tavkar and David J. Hansen,

"Interventions for Families Victimized by Child Sexual Abuse: Clinical Issues and Approaches for Child Advocacy Center-Based Services," *Aggression and Violent Behavior* 16, no. 3 (2011): 188–199, https://doi.org/10.1016/j.avb.2011.02.005.

16. Tavkar and Hansen, "Interventions for Families Victimized by Child Sexual Abuse"; and Teresa L. Young and Debra Nelson-Gardell, "A Grounded Theory Study of Collaboration in Multidisciplinary Teams," *Journal of Public Child Welfare* 12, no. 5 (2018): 576–595, https://doi.org/10.1080/15548732.2018.1436112.

17. Our research team included Mary ("Mara") J. Waller, PhD, Matthew McGlone, PhD, Ana Aguilar, MA, Dina Inman Ramgolam, PhD, Dron Mandhana, PhD, and Estee Solomon Gray, MBA, MSEE.

18. Kathleen M. Eisenhardt, "Building Theories from Case Study Research," *The Academy of Management Review* 14, no. 4 (1989): 532–550.

19. Grant McCracken, *The Long Interview* (Sage, 1988).

20. Don A. Dillman, Jolene D. Smyth, and Melani Christian, *Internet, Phone, Mail, and Mixed-Mode Surveys: The Tailored Design* (John Wiley, 2014).

21. Joanna Sheridan, Kerry Chamberlain, and Ann Dupuis, "Timelining: Visualizing Experience," *Qualitative Research* 11, no. 5 (2011): 552–569.

22. We offered the following instructions: Please take a blank sheet of paper. I would like for you to draw a horizontal line just like the one on the screen and then anchor each side; the left side will have a short vertical line, which indicates the starting point and the far right side has an arrow. Now take a couple of minutes and use this timeline to indicate what the sequence of events looked like for your last case—not the hypothetical we just discussed but your last actual case. Make sure and indicate what your unit of time is and use words to describe each line you mark on the continuous, horizontal line. In other words, please feel free to draw and mark what the MDT process looked like for you during your last case.

23. Dawna I. Ballard and David R. Seibold, "Time Orientation and Temporal Variation Across Work Groups: Implications for Group and Organizational Communication," *Western Journal of Communication* 64, no. 2 (2000): 218–242.

24. Zerubavel, *Hidden Rhythms*.

25. David S. Landes, *Revolution in Time: Clocks and the Making of the Modern World* (Harvard University Press, 1984).

26. Ginny Sprang et al., "Defining Secondary Traumatic Stress and Developing Targeted Assessments and Interventions: Lessons Learned from Research and Leading Experts," *Traumatology* 25, no. 2 (2019): 72.

27. We computed a team-level measure of participation for each MDT by asking each respondent to report their percentage attendance in case reviews. These

individual responses were then aggregated and divided by the number of members in the respective MDT location.

28. First, a simple linear regression was used to check whether MDT members' average participation in case reviews predicts team performance. A significant regression equation was found [$F(1, 66) = 8.49$, $p = 0.005$], with an R^2 of 0.114 (adjusted $R^2 = 0.101$). Results indicate that with every 1 percent increase in MDT members' average participation in case reviews, MDT performance increases by 0.012 units. Another simple linear regression was conducted to check if MDT members' average participation in case reviews predicts satisfaction with interprofessional communication. Results indicate that interprofessional communication is significantly predicted by MDT members' average participation in case reviews [$F(1, 66) = 24.25$, $p = 0.001$, $R^2 = 0.27$] (adjusted $R^2 = 0.26$). Furthermore, results suggest that with every 1 percent increase in MDT members' average participation in case reviews, MDT members' satisfaction with interprofessional communication increases by 0.022 units. Finally, we conducted a mediation analysis using PROCESS to test whether MDT members' interprofessional communication mediated the relationship between MDT members' average participation in case reviews and MDT teams' performance. In step 1 of the mediation model, which ignores the mediator, results indicate that the average participation in case reviews ($b = 0.012$, $SE = 0.004$, $p = 0.005$) was a significant predictor of satisfaction with interprofessional communication ($R^2 = 0.114$). Step 2 showed that the regression of MDT members' average participation in case reviews on the mediator, interprofessional communication, was also significant ($b = 0.022$, $SE = 0.004$, $p = 0.0001$; $R^2 = 0.269$). Step 3 of the mediation process showed that the mediator (interprofessional communication), controlling for MDT team members' average participation in case reviews, was a significant predictor of team performance ($b = 0.62$, $SE = 0.081$, $p = 0.0001$; $R^2 = 0.534$). Step 4 of the analysis revealed that upon controlling for the mediator (interprofessional communication), MDT team members' average participation in case reviews was no longer a significant predictor of team performance ($b = -0.002$, $SE = 0.003$, $p = 0.578$), consistent with full mediation. These mediation results suggest that interprofessional communication mediates the positive relationship between an MDT's participation in case reviews and their performance. Specifically, with every 1 percent increase in MDT members' average participation in case reviews, MDT performance increases by 0.62 units.

29. This theme emerged in chapter 3 and is often required to bolster misplaced fast CDLs.

30. Dennis W. Organ, "Organizational Citizenship Behavior: The Good Soldier Syndrome," (Lexington Books/DC Healthy and Co., 1988), 4.

31. Shelly L. Jackson, "Results from the Virginia Multidisciplinary Team Knowledge and Functioning Survey: The Importance of Differentiating by Groups Affiliated with a Child Advocacy Center," *Children and Youth Services Review* 34, no. 7 (2012): 1243–1250.

Chapter 5

1. Entire literatures in communication and linguistics account for the fundamental indeterminacy of language. Nonetheless, we are language-using animals, and it is the most efficient communication tool at our disposal.

2. Nelson and Stolterman, *The Design Way*, 12.

3. Nelson and Stolterman, *The Design Way*, 192.

4. Ian Fleming Zhou and Jo-Ansie van Wyk, "North Korea's Entrapment and Time Delay Tactics During Nuclear Negotiations," *Asian Journal of Peacebuilding* 9, no. 2 (2021): 411–426, https://doi.org/10.18588/202108.00a105.

5. Troy A. Murphy, "American Political Mythology and the Senate Filibuster," *Argumentation and Advocacy* 32, no. 2 (1995): 90–107, https://doi.org/10.1080/00028533 .1995.11977983.

6. Caitlin M. Mulcahy, Diana C. Parry, and Troy D. Glover, "The 'Patient': The Trauma of Waiting and the Power of Resistance for People Living with Cancer," *Qualitative Health Research* 20, no. 8 (2010): 1062–1075, https://doi.org/10.1177 /1049732310369139.

7. Barbara J. O'Keefe, "The Logic of Message Design: Individual Differences in Reasoning About Communication," *Communication Monographs* 55, no. 1 (1988): 80–103, https://doi.org/10.1080/03637758809376159, p. 85.

8. Carl DiSalvo, *Adversarial Design* (MIT Press, 2015).

9. Taylor, *Scientific Management*.

10. John S. Hassard, "Rethinking the Hawthorne Studies: The Western Electric Research in its Social, Political and Historical Context," *Human Relations* 65, no. 11 (2012): 1431–1461, https://doi.org/10.1177/0018726712452168.

11. Joel Spring, *American Education* (Routledge, 2019).

12. Linda L. Morse and Diane D. Allensworth, "Placing Students at the Center: The Whole School, Whole Community, Whole Child Model," *Journal of School Health* 85, no. 11 (2015): 785–794.

13. Kathryn Dill, "Teachers Are Quitting, and Companies Are Hot to Hire Them," *The Wall Street Journal*, February 2, 2022, https://www.wsj.com/articles/teachers-are -quitting-and-companies-are-hot-to-hire-them-11643634181.

14. Erika L. Kirby and Kathleen Krone, "'The Policy Exists but You Can't Really Use It': Communication and the Structuration of Work–Family Policies," *Journal of Applied Communication Research* 30, no. 1 (2002): 50–77.

15. At the time this book went to press, more than two years after our meeting, the undeveloped property still sat empty, having been on the market nearly a year.

16. Hall, *The Dance of Life*.

17. Nelson and Stolterman, *The Design Way*, 192.

18. James Hillman, *The Soul's Code: In Search of Character and Calling* (Ballantine Books, 2017).

19. Nelson and Stolterman, *The Design Way*, 21.

20. Nelson and Stolterman, *The Design Way*, 18.

21. This "right" time is called "kairos." For more, see Phillip Sipiora and James S. Baumlin, *Rhetoric and Kairos: Essays in History, Theory, and Praxis* (SUNY Press, 2002).

22. Gilly Leshed, Maria Håkansson, and Joseph "Jofish" Kaye, "'Our Life Is the Farm and Farming Is Our Life': Home–Work Coordination in Organic Farm Families," in *Proceedings of the 17th ACM Conference on Computer Supported Cooperative Work and Social Computing* (ACM, 2014), 487–498, https://doi.org/10.1145/2531602.2531708.

Chapter 6

1. Nelson and Stolterman, *The Design Way*.

2. Bourdieu, *Outline of a Theory of Practice*.

3. Michelle-Linh T. Nguyen, Samuel V. Schotland, and Joel D. Howell, "From Individualized Interactions to Standardized Schedules: A History of Time Organization in US Outpatient Medicine," *Annals of Internal Medicine* 175, no. 10 (2022): 1468–1474.

4. Natalia Besedovsky, Fritz-Julius Grafe, Hanna Hilbrandt, and Hannes Langguth, "Time as Infrastructure: For an Analysis of Contemporary Urbanization," *City* 23, no. 4–5 (2019): 580–588, https://doi.org/10.1080/13604813.2019.1689726.

5. At the most broad and technical level, a time-based infrastructure includes the basic timekeeping technologies that allow these organizational and institutional practices to occur. In the United States, this time-based infrastructure is overseen by the National Institute of Standards and Technology (NIST).

6. Brown, *Change by Design*, 73.

7. Christine M. Beckman and Melissa Mazmanian, *Dreams of the Overworked* (Stanford University Press, 2020).

8. Jeanine W. Turner, *Being Present: Commanding Attention at Work (and at Home) by Managing Your Social Presence* (Georgetown University Press, 2022), 2.

9. Jocelyn Spence, Dimitrios Darzentasa, Harriet Cameron, et al., "Gifting in Museums: Using Multiple Time Orientations to Heighten Present-Moment Engagement,"

Human–Computer Interaction 37, no. 2 (2022): 180–210, https://doi.org/10.1080/07370024.2021.1923496.

10. Jocelyn Spence, Dimitrios Darzentasa, Harriet Cameron, et al., "Gifting in Museums: Using Multiple Time Orientations to Heighten Present-Moment Engagement," *Human–Computer Interaction* 37, no. 2 (2022): 181, https://doi.org/10.1080/07370024.2021.1923496.

11. Ilana Graetz, Jie Huang, Emilie Muelly, Anjali Gopalan, and Mary E. Reed, "Primary Care Visits Are Timelier When Patients Choose Telemedicine: A Cross-Sectional Observational Study," *Telemedicine and e-Health* 28, no. 9 (2022): 1374–1378.

12. Reem Alkilany, Yasir Tarabichi, and Raymond Hong, "Telemedicine Visits During Covid-19 Improved Clinic Show Rates," *ACR Open Rheumatology* 4, no. 2 (2022): 136–141.

13. S. Ayca Erdogan, Tracey L. Krupski, and Jennifer Mason Lobo, "Optimization of Telemedicine Appointments in Rural Areas," *Service Science* 10, no. 3 (2018): 261–276.

14. Ali Roghani and Samin Panahi, "Does Telemedicine Reduce Health Disparities? Longitudinal Evidence During the COVID-19 Pandemic in the US," *medRxiv* (2021): 2021–03.

15. Weick and Sutcliffe, *Managing the Unexpected*, 22.

16. Weber, *The Protestant Ethic and the Spirit of Capitalism*.

Index

Aakhus, Mark, 11–12, 15, 53, 58
Adam, Barbara, 51
Adaptation
    as improvisational, 29
    as outside of time pressure, 29
    as phase of action, 29
    "time-out" period, 29
    transcendent approach, 29
Africa, 114
"Agile at 20: The Failed Rebellion"
    (blog post), 119
"Agile Is Dead (Long Live Agility)"
    (blog post), 119
Agile methodology, 115
    theory of communication, 118–119
Agile Software Development, 116–117,
    120, 169
    fast communication, inconsistent
    with, 119
    "mushy stuff," 118–119
    nonlinear trajectory, 119
    organizational anarchists, 118
Aguilar, Ana, 45
Albert, Stuart, 36
Amazonization, 112, 179

American football, 91, 112
    being "hurt" versus "injured,"
        distinction between, 101–102
    coal mining analogy, 100–101
    communication-as-design, as fast
        CDL, 97–98
    communication process, 94–95
    fast design logic, 95, 99, 101–102
    as glamorized, 93
    identity development, 94–96
    as last "gladiator sport," 93
    medical care, 101
    present-focused, 101
    single frame of interaction, focus
        on, 98
    timescape of, 92
    as transactional, 99
    transcendence through human
        interaction, 99
Analog approach
    agrarian sensibility, 163–164
    holistic approach of, 163
    presence, inviting of, 163
    task accomplishment, 163–164
Anthropocene, 38

Anthropocene Working Group, 38
Anti-exhaustion wristwatch (monitor naps taken, long meals shared, climbing nothing, dream rate, and more) (Makonnen), 6
Apple
  Focus setting, 48
Asia, 114
Augustus, 165
Availability, 13–14, 32, 47, 61, 125, 146
  constant, 140, 143–144
  informal collaboration, 141
  "open-door" policy, 48
  real-time, 134
  shared, 140–141
  telemedicine, 176–177

Baby Boomers, 105–107
Bandwidth tax, 87–88
Barbour, Joshua, 140
Barge, Kevin, 140
Bastian, Michelle, 51
Beckman, Christine, 171
Behavioral reform, 158
Being Present (Turner), 172
Benedictine monks, 136
Big Medium art gallery, 5
Bluedorn, Allen, 45–46
Bourdieu, Pierre, 13
Bradshaw, Terry, 100
Breslin, Maggie, 53–54
Brown, Tim, 65, 167
  divergence and convergence, 171–172
  prototyping, 66
Bruneau, Thomas, 12
Burnout, 10, 57, 89–90, 137

Calendar, 5
  availability, 13–14
  expressive quality of, 12–13
Center for Child Protection, 180

Center for Sports Communication and Media, 94. *See also* Texas Program in Sports and Media
Chaplin, Charlie, 112
Chat option, 112
Child abuse, 120, 129–130, 134, 138–139, 143, 148, 174–175
  disciplines, 121–126, 135–136
Child protective services (CPS), 122–123, 125, 132, 140–141, 158
  overburdened, 142
  turnover rates, 137
Children's advocacy center (CAC) movement, 63, 120, 134, 137, 140, 161, 167, 169, 174–175
  child abuse, 148
  collaboration and information sharing, 121–122, 127–129
  complementarity of fast and slow CDL, 144
  complementary chronemic theories, reliance on, 121–122
  MDTs, 121–126, 128–129, 133, 135–136
Children's Advocacy Centers of Texas (CACTX), 86, 112, 115, 123–125, 127, 135, 167, 172–173, 180
  collaboration, 129
  communicate slow to go fast, theory of communication of, 128–129
  fast and slow CDLs, in complementary fashion, 134, 142–143
  growth and success of, 174
  "how" of, 128
  information sharing, 129
  MDT Enhancement Program, 174–175
  Outcome Measurement System, 175
  overwork, 143
  slow CDL, based on, 142, 147

Statewide Intake Initiative (SWI), 174–175
systemic problem of, 142
"what" of, 128
"why" of, 128
Chronemic design, 16, 81, 93, 101–102, 150, 152–153, 169, 171
bandwidth tax, 88
complementarity, 175, 178
fast, 72
fidelity, reliance on, 175–176, 178
ideation, 167
implementation, 167, 169
inconsistencies, 170
inspiration, 167
iteration, reliance on, 166–167
mindful organizing, 179
processual (temporal) nature of, 63
slow, 72
task accomplishment, 115
timescale, 91
time-sensitive task accomplishment, 166–167
Chronemic Design Toolkit, 16, 35, 167, 170, 181–182
Chronemics, 2, 67–68, 104
defining of, 12
Chronemic theories, 103, 181
chronemic theory of organization, 76
Chronemic urgency, 104
high, 107
interaction, as transactional, 110
low, 107
media, 108
phone calls, 106–107
responsiveness imperative, 110
text messages, 106–107
Chronic traumatic encephalopathy (CTE), 92–93
Cinema
as metaphor for frames and framing communication, 34

Civic engagement, 154–155
Classical school of management, 19–20, 68
resistance to, 156–157
time-and-motion studies, 69
Clocks, 1–2, 5, 8, 50, 114
alarm clocks, 163–164
around-the-clock, 129
atomic, 4
biological, 3–4, 164
digital, 163
timeliness, clock-based aspect, 117
Collaboration, 121, 122, 127, 146
around-the-clock, 140
formal MDT (scheduled), 129, 134–136
informal MDT (real time), 129–130, 134, 141
real-time availability, 134
scheduling, 134
time-based assumptions, 134
time-based practices, 134
Collective communication design, 140
MDTs, 144, 146
Communication, 11, 16, 32, 53, 66
amount of time, 20
competing theories of, 89–90
complementarity, 175
design, 107
fast logics, 68
fast theories of, 68, 80, 84
fitting around existing time constraints, 17
making room for temporal processes, 18
multiple time frames, 23
organizational, 42
relationships, as central to getting work done, 20
speed, 67–68
team members, 25

Communication (cont.)
theories of, 33, 72–73, 76, 94–95,
128–129, 156–158, 161, 175, 179
time, relationship between, 12, 14,
19–20, 67–68
time frame for interaction, 21
trauma, 24–25
Communication-as-design, 11, 16, 29,
34–35, 66, 84, 86, 107, 141, 150,
152, 160
building relationships, 15
collective time, 14
in health care, 54
managed-care visits, as transactional,
30
multiple streams of digital
communication, 104
task completion, 26
as theoretical perspective, 10
theories of communication, 156
and time, 12, 31–32
time dimensions, 63
timescale, 39–40, 63
timescape, 51–52
Communication design logics (CDLs),
89, 171. *See also* fast
communication design,
slow communication design
of drive-through restaurants, 39
of fine dining establishments, 39
linear approach, 25–26
multiple time frames, drawing on, 24
nonlinear approach, 25
pause, 18
speed, preoccupation with, 18
time-based assumptions, 44
Communication media, 1
Communication process, 86, 94–95, 105
time dimensions, 35, 42
timescale of, 35, 41–42
Communication setting
underlying process, 40–41

Competing theories of communication,
89–90
Complementarity, 175, 178–179, 181
Complementary theories of
communication, 66, 151, 156, 159
Comprehensive Framework for
Chronemic Design, 181
Concurrency, 48, 61
Corporate sabotage, 157
COVID-19, 5, 8, 78
lockdown, 86
Great Resignation, 91
Criminal justice agencies, 120
Csikszentmihalyi, Mihaly
flow, concept of, 28
Cyberinfrastructure, 15, 26

Deadlines, 1, 4
Delay, 62
punctuality, 50–51
Design, 3
communication, as natural fact
about, 107
as hypotheses, 11, 16, 53
"measure twice, cut once," 3
as natural fact about communication,
11, 15–16, 31–32
objectivity, 37
subjective judgments, 37
as theoretical, 11, 16
Design culture, 162, 180
design wisdom, reliance on, 179
uncertainty, embracing of, 179
Design logics, 54
Design Studio (magazine), 10
Design thinking, 161
analog approach, 162
Design way, 151
Design wisdom, 152, 162
analog versus digital thinking,
163
design culture, 179

making room for transcendent
interaction, 161
temporality, attention to, 163
Design work
designers, 11, 16, 53, 155, 166, 171,
181
temporal aspects of, 6, 10
Digital communication, 104–106, 108,
111–112, 114–115, 121–122, 158,
162–164, 169, 173, 180
Digital technologies
Agile methodology, 115
time-based focus that excludes
temporal processes, 114–115
Dillman Survey Methodology, 126
DiSalvo, Carl
adversarial design, 153
Dreams of the Overworked (Beckman and
Mazmanian), 171
Durkheim, Emile, 12

Edwards, Dr. Harry, 92
Eisenberg, Eric, 29
jamming, concept of, 28
transcendence, 173
Email, 20, 104, 106, 108–109
Eriksen, Thomas Hylland, 10
Europe, 39, 114

Face time, 49
Fast communication design, 2, 16–18,
21, 25, 51, 53–54, 56, 60, 63, 66,
73, 86, 95, 104, 112, 119, 149–152,
157, 177–178
aim of, 68
in American football, 97–102
complementarity of, 181–182
as default design for interactions, 111
efficiency of, 110–111
employee manuals, 20
of everyday digital communication,
108

facilitating coordination, 110–111
framing, 34
Great Resignation, 69
high chronemic urgency, 107
interaction, as transactional, 27–28, 85
linear approach, 26, 28, 71, 85, 114
misused, 71–72
present-focused, 101, 108–109
scheduling, 88
shape of trajectory between time and
interaction, 33
short customer service calls, and brief
doctor's visits, 20
single frame, oriented to, 23, 28, 71,
84, 108–109, 114
slow communication design, as
complementary, 3, 72, 110, 121,
134, 142–144, 146, 167, 169, 176
slower communication, leading to, 20
speed, 68, 87, 167
speed of action, 32
task accomplishment, 68, 115
as thriving, 72
time-based infrastructure, as how,
170
time dimensions, 34–35
as time focused, 110
time frame, of interaction, 23, 33
timescale, 34–35
time-sensitive communication,
indispensable for, 102–103
transactional relationships, 71, 114
transcendence, 110
what interaction offers, 33
workplace norms, 71
Fast food, 112
Ferris, Stephen
depth of field, 46
Fictive schedule, 77–78
Flexibility, 49, 62, 88–89, 134, 140
informal collaboration, 141
Flow, 28

Framing
    as creative tool, 34–35
    zoom and focus, 42, 63
France, 42
Friedman, Meyer, 45
Future time focus, 46–47, 87, 134

Generation X, 105
Generation Z, 105–108
Gill, Rebecca, 140
Going slow to go fast, 66, 165, 173, 181
Good design, 164
    "Measure twice, cut once" proverb,
        165–166
Google Maps, 50
Google N-gram
    "more-faster-better," 2
Great Resignation, 91, 158
    fast communication design logics, 69

Hall, Edward T., 1, 113–115, 161
Hall, Jeffrey C., 3
Health care, 42, 54–56, 58–59, 62–63,
        78, 82–85, 101, 152, 169–170, 176,
        179–180 timescape, 53, 61
    as time-sensitive, 79–81
High reliability organizations
    mindful organizing, 178–179
Highsmith, Jim, 118
Hillman, James, 162
Human relations school of management,
    157
    suggestion boxes, 160

Ideation, 65–66, 166–167, 169–171, 181
Identification, 94
Implementation, 66, 68, 166–167,
        169–171, 175, 181
Inclusion, 18, 64
Inconsistent theories of communication,
    73
    bait and switch, 76

Industrial capitalism, 44
Industrialization, 10, 18, 112
Industrial Revolution, 19–20, 69, 115,
    156
Information sharing, 121–122, 127, 143
    efficiency, 135, 144
    forensic interviewer timeline, 132
    pace of, 134–135
    time-based assumptions, 134
    time-based practices, 134
    timescale, 129–130, 132
Innovation, 167
    ideation, 65–66
    implementation, 65–66
    inspiration, 65
    multi-space, 65
Inspiration, 65–66, 166–167, 170–171,
    181
Interaction, 30, 110, 113, 119, 150, 152,
    157
    deep work, 111
    everyday "friction," loss of, 111
    fast communication design, as
        default choice, 111
    interaction work, 20
    linear approach, 26, 85
    multiple time frames, 147, 158
    nonlinear approach, 26
    present focus, 108–109
    relationships, 27
    school-based, 158
    single frame, 98, 108–109
    speed, single-minded pursuit of,
        160–161
    subjective qualities, 59–60
    and time, 98, 109
    time frame of, 21, 32, 108–109
    timescale, 60
    time-sensitive, 153
    as transactional, 27, 110, 155–156
    as transcendent, 27–29, 31, 99,
        160–161

unplanned conversations, 26–27
as wasteful, 155–156
Interpretation, 64–65
Ishak, Andrew, 29
Iteration, 166

Jackson, Sally, 11, 15
Jamming
collective action, 28
transcendence, 28
Johnson, Jimmy, 99

Kalman, Yoram, 45, 104–105
Kee, Kerk, 27, 29, 119
building trusting relationships, 14–16
nonlinear communication, 26
virtual organizations, and colocated
meetings, 14–15
Kenya, 42

Landry, Tom, 99
Leshed, Gilly, 163–164
Lifespan
of professionals, 91–92
Linearity, 32, 173
Linear relationship, 2–3, 8, 14, 25–26,
28, 58, 71, 85, 99–100, 103, 109,
112, 114, 135–136, 157, 165, 174
Lott, Ronnie, 98

Makonnen, Betelhem, 4–6, 16, 163
Malaysia, 42
Malicious obedience, 157
Mandhana, Dron, 26–27
Manifesto for Agile Software
Development, 169
Mayo Clinic, 53–54
Mazmanian, Melissa, 171
McDonaldization, 112, 179
McDonald's, 112
McGlone, Matthew, 123–124
McKinsey Global Institute, 20

McMahon, Jim, 100–101
Medicare, 80, 84
Message design logic, 107–108
Millennials, 105
Mindful organizing, 178–179
Modern Times (film), 112
Montori, Dr. Victor, 53, 56–61, 79–80, 90
communication-as-design, in
health care, 54, 62–63
unhurried, 54–55
M-time (monochromic) cultures, 113
as linear, 114
single-frame focus, 114
task accomplishment, 114
as transactional, 114
Mullainathan, Sendhil, 45, 88
bandwidth tax, 87
Multidisciplinary teams (MDTs), 15,
132–133, 138–139, 156, 172–175
burnout, reducing of, 137
child abuse disciplines, 121–126,
135–136
collaboration, 129–130, 146
collaboration and information
sharing, 127–128
collective communication design,
140, 144, 146
competing chronemic designs, 146
complementarity of fast and slow
CDL, 144, 146
constant availability, 140, 144, 146
difficult work, 145
fast pace, and time-sensitive
information sharing, 143
flexibility, 140
function of, 130
"grand-tour" questions, 125
incongruity, 142
information sharing, efficiency of,
144
interaction through multiple time
frames, 147

nonlinear relationship between communication and time, 147
presence, 173
secondary trauma, 144–146
scheduling and prioritizing, 143–144
slow communication design, 147–148
temporal symmetry, 136
timescape, 147
transcendence, 139, 146–147
turnover, 145–146
underfunded, 145
understaffing, 141
urgency, 140–141

National Aeronautics and Space Administration (NASA), 51
National Collegiate Athletic Association (NCAA), 92, 96
fast design logic, 95
slow design logic, 95
National Football League (NFL), 92–94, 96–98
concussion lawsuit, 101
fast design logic, 95, 102
linear relationship, 99
"Not for Long," 100
National Institute for Occupational Safety and Health, 92
Nelson, Harold G., 157, 163, 172
design way, 151
design wisdom, 6, 162
interpretation, description of, 64–65
Netherlands, 39, 59
Nguyen, Dr. Michelle-Linh, 179–180
Nonlinearity, 157, 166, 177
Nonlinear relationship, 3, 8, 15, 25–26, 28–29, 57–58, 81, 99–100, 111, 113–114, 119–120, 147, 153, 155, 158, 165, 167, 170, 174

Office Space (film), 154
O'Keefe, Barbara, 153
Optics
depth of field, 46
Organizational theory, 68
reductive approach, 167
Organizations
external stakeholders, 73
internal stakeholders, 73
Outline of a Theory of Practice (Bourdieu), 13

Past, present, and future, 44–45, 61
Past time focus, 46–47
Patient Revolution (PR), 53–54, 56–57, 169
availability, 61
concurrent, 61
delay, 62
flexibility, 62
pace, 62
past, present, and future, 61
punctuality, 61
scarcity, 61
scheduling, 62
urgency, 62
Pauling, Linus, 171
Perceived shape of trajectory between time and interaction, 57–58
Petrini, Carlo, 19
Phoenix Children's Hospital, 24
Portugal, 42
Power of Now, The (Tolle), 149
Precision, 64, 163
Presence, 172–173
through analog, 163
Present time focus, 47, 101, 108–109
Process-based practices, 55–56
Professional socialization, 40, 75, 90, 94–95, 97–98
Prototyping, 66
Pschetz, Larissa, 51

P-time (polychromic) cultures, 114–115
    interactions, 113
Public schools, 158
Punctuality, 61
    delay, 50–51

Qualtrics survey, 126

Rafaeli, Sheizaf, 105
Rate busting, 157
Real-time communication, 105–106
Recursivity, 12
Reductive thinking
    digital approach, 162
Relationship development, 19
Ritzer, George, 179
    calculability, 112
    control, 112
    efficiency, 112
    predictability, 112
Rock Standard Time (RST) (Makonnen),
    4–6, 8, 23, 163
Rosbash, Michael, 3
Rosenman, Ray, 45

Sabelis, Ida
    flower analogy, 40–42
    zoom and focus, 36, 40
Sarkar, Dr. Urmimala, 77, 176
Scarcity, 44–45, 49, 61, 89
    as changing how we think, 87
Scheduling, 49–50, 62
    prioritizing, 143–144
    temporal symmetry, 136
Scientific Management (Taylor), 69–71,
    156
Scorsese, Martin, 33–36
Secondary trauma, 136, 144–146
Seibold, David, 153–156
Shafir, Eldar, 45, 88
    bandwidth tax, 87
Silent Language, The (Hall), 1

Silicon Valley, 102
    culture of disruption, 46
    meal-replacement drinks, 111
    pain point, 111
Skype, 15
Slow
    as scarce resource, 10
    as term, 19
Slow communication design, 2, 16–18,
    25, 51, 53–54, 56, 60, 63, 66, 73,
    88, 95, 102–104, 108, 119–120,
    145, 149, 151, 156, 159, 161
    aim of, 68
    "bad" name, 153
    challenges to, 173–181
    complementarity of, 181–182
    cultivate design culture, 179–181
    delay tactics, as inconsistent with,
        153
    design for complementarity, 175–179
    distinctive power of, 147–148
    divergence and convergence, 172
    extraction model, as inconsistent
        with, 160
    fast communication design, as
        complementary, 3, 72, 110, 121,
        134, 142–144, 146, 167, 169, 176
    flexibility, 89
    framing, 34
    future-focused lens, 87, 97
    health care, equitable access to, 170
    how design works, 19, 170
    importance of, 152
    interaction, as transcending value of
        known resources, 27
    meeting resistance to, 173–175
    as meta-competency, 166, 174
    multiple time frames, supporting of,
        28, 111, 113
    nonlinear approach, 26, 28, 111,
        113, 155
    presence, 172

Slow communication design (cont.)
  relationships, as how of, 170
  rush to certainty, running contrary
    to, 166
  scheduling, 89
  shape of trajectory between time and
    interaction, 33
  slow movement, distinct from,
    19
  speed of action, 32
  task accomplishment, as original
    means of, 113, 115, 170
  temporality, 150
  time frame, of interaction, 23, 33
  transcendence, 111, 113, 155
  as unhurried, 55
  "went slow to go fast," 89
  what interaction offers, 33
Slow design, 19
Slow food movement, 19
Slow movement, 19
Slow science, 19
Smith, Cherise, 5
Snapchat, 107–108
Social media, 104
Social service agencies, 120
Software development industry,
  116–117
Spain, 42
Spence, Jocelyn, 172
Spring, Joel, 158
Stolterman, Erik, 6, 15, 172
  design way, 151
  design wisdom, 162
  interpretation, description of,
    64–65
Su, Dr. Lillian, 24
Subcommission on Quaternary
  Stratigraphy, 38
Sutcliffe, Kathleen, 178–179
Symbols
  efficiency of, 1

Task accomplishment
  analog approach, 163–164
  chronemic design, 115
  fast CDLs, 68
  in M-time cultures, 114
  slow CDLs, 113
  time, 111–112
  relationships, as primary means of,
    116, 118, 170
  time-sensitive, 166–167, 174
Task specifications
  approach of, 115
  contours of, 115
  purpose of, 115
Taylor, Frederick, 70–71, 156
  time-and-motion studies, 69
Telemedicine, 176–178
Telepresence robots, 14
Temporality, 4, 6, 30, 54, 65, 67
  biological, bringing time into
    alignment, 3
  of care, 170
  design wisdom, 163
  of phenomenon, 36–37, 52–53
  of rocks, 5
  speed, 117
  temporal landmarks, 111
  time, distinction between, 8, 10–11,
    13, 32, 35, 58, 117, 150
Temporal processes
  focus and zoom, 36, 40, 42
Texas Program in Sports and Media,
  94. See also Center for Sports
  Communication and Media
Theories of communication, 94–95, 105
  of patient care, 79
Three features of a timescape, 169
Three realities of chronemic design,
  170–-171
Three signposts to support chronemic
  design, 170–171
Three specifications of a task, 170

Three theories of communication, 167
Time, 1–3, 51, 53, 166–167
  of activity, as fungible marker, 6
  availability, 13–14, 32
  calendars, 5, 12
  collective time, 14
  colocated activities, 14–15
  as commodity that can be saved or
    spent, 108
  communication, relationship between,
    12, 14, 19–20, 25–26, 67–68
  communication-as-design, 12, 31–32
  as core level of culture, 161
  cyberstructure, 26
  delay, 32
  designable features of, 32, 67
  as everyday communication, 13
  experience of, 42, 44
  flexibility, 32
  interaction, 21, 25, 32, 58, 98, 109
  keeping someone waiting, 14
  labor, tied to, 111–112
  linearity, 32
  linear relationships, 25, 103, 109
  as multidimensional, 51
  multiple time frames, 25
  nonlinear relationships, 25, 113
  pace, 32
  past, present, and future focus, 32,
    44–45
  presence and absence, 13
  punctuality, 32
  recursivity, 12
  reminder alarms, 4
  scarcity, 32, 44–45, 49
  scheduling, 32, 49–50
  speed, 67–68
  as symbolic marker, 149
  task accomplishment, primary
    means of, 18, 111
  temporality, distinction between, 8,
    10–11, 13, 32, 35, 58, 117, 150

  time dimensions, 59
  timescale, 59
  as tool, 150
  urgency, 32, 44–45
  work, 8
  wristwatch, looking at as common
    gesture, 14
Time-based assumptions, 82–84, 134, 150
  future time focus, 46–47
  media, 106
  past time focus, 46
  present time focus, 47
  responsiveness imperative, 106
  scarcity, 44–45
  time-sensitive responsiveness, 106
  urgency, 45
  urgency, culturally-based assumptions,
    106
Time-based interventions
  speed, as reductive, 68
Time-based practices, 55–56, 83–86, 134,
  150
  availability, 47–48
  concurrency, 47–48
  culturally-based assumptions, 106
  delay, 47, 50
  flexibility, 47, 49, 82
  pace, 47–48
  punctuality, 47, 50
  scheduling, 47, 49
  time-sensitive responsiveness, 106
Time dimensions, 34, 44, 59, 63, 89
  of communication process, 35
Time frames, 3
  of interactions, 24, 32, 57
  multiple, 23–25, 28, 157
  time and interaction, shifting of, 25
Time-keeping devices, 8
Time-keeping technologies
  calendars, 1
  clocks, 1–2
  schedules, 1

Timeless time, 8
Timeliness
    clock-based aspect of, 117
Timelining, 130
Timescale, 34, 51, 59, 63, 68, 80–81, 89,
    150
    brief, 95–96
    child protective services timeline,
        131–132
    of communication process, 35, 41–42
    culture, role of, 39, 41
    definition of, 36
    demonstrating mastery of being
        professional, 95
    of design effort, 35
    efficiency of chronemic design, 91
    family advocate timeline, 131, 133
    fiscal year, 38, 40
    forensic interviewer timeline,
        131–132
    geological, 37–38
    information sharing, 129–130, 132
    law enforcement timeline, 131, 133
    long, 95
    medical professional timeline,
        131–132
    objective and subjective, intersection
        of, 37–42, 44
    of patient care, 81
    of phenomenon, 36, 38–40, 42, 60
    shared understanding, 38
    therapist timeline, 131, 133
    of time-sensitive responsiveness,
        105–106
    unhurried conversations, 59–60
Timescape, 51–52, 59, 66, 77, 147, 152,
    172–173
    of American football, 92
    communication process, 72–73
    of everyday digital communication,
        as fast CDL, 108
    flexibility, 134

    future, 134
    of health care, 61
    time dimensions, 72
    timescale, 72
    urgency, 134
Time-sensitive responsiveness
    context, 107–108
    not responding in timely fashion, as
        rude, 107–108
    response zones, 105
    time-based assumptions and prac-
        tices, 106
    timescale, 105–106
Time shadowing, 78, 83
    debriefing interview, 79
    ethnographic notes, 79
Time studies, 36
Tolle, Eckhart, 149
Tortoise and the Hare, The (Aesop), 165
Transactional communication, 112
    in American football, 99
    as fast CDL, 114
    interaction, 110
    as limited compromise within
        perceived time limits, 28
    linear approach, 28
Transcendence, 30, 110, 153, 155, 157,
    160, 173, 177
    adaptation, 29
    design wisdom, 161
    interaction, 27–28, 99, 160–161
    jamming, as hallmark of, 28
    MDTs, 139, 146–147
    slow communication design, 111,
        113
Transcendent communication, 30–31
    going beyond perceived time limit, 28
    nonlinear approach, 28
Transcendent interaction, 28, 31
    as distracted by time pressure, 29
Turner, Jeanine, 172
    presence, 173

Turner, Robert W., 94
Type A behavior, 98
  "hurry sickness," 45

United Kingdom, 39
United States, 39, 114, 103, 148,
  174–175
United States Naval Observatory
  Master Clock, 50
  Time Services, 50
University of California San Francisco,
  77
University of Maastricht, 39
University of Texas, 11, 94, 104
Unplanned conversations, 26
  value of, 27
*Untitled (anti-productivity exercises
  or moving time and space)*
  (Makonnen), 6
*Untitled (our misunderstanding of time, of
  ourselves)* (Makonnen), 8
Urgency, 44–45, 62, 109, 134, 140
  culturally-based assumptions, 106
  deep work, 111
  informal collaboration, 141

Videoconferencing, 14–15

Waller, Mary "Mara," 124
Weber, Max
  iron cage, 10, 179–180
Weick, Karl, 178–179
WhatsApp, 108
"Whole student," 158
Why We Revolt (Montori), 61–63,
  79–80
Wooden, John, 18, 165
Work–life balance
  lack of complementarity, 158–159

Young, Michael W., 3

Zaheer, Akbar, 36
Zaheer, Srilata, 36
Zappos, 48
Zerubavel, Eviatar, 136
  temporal landmarks, 111
Zuckerberg, Mark
  "move fast and break things" slogan,
  67, 93, 99–100

Publisher contact:
The MIT Press
Massachusetts Institute of Technology
77 Massachusetts Avenue, Cambridge, MA 02139
mitpress.mit.edu

EU Authorised Representative:
Easy Access System Europe, Mustamäe tee 50,
10621 Tallinn, Estonia
gpsr.requests@easproject.com

Printed by Integrated Books International,
United States of America